Making Sense of Children's Thinking and Behavior

A Step-by-Step Tool for Understanding Children with NLD, Asperger's, HFA, PDD-NOS, and other Neurological Disorders

Leslie Holzhauser-Peters and Leslie True

Jessica Kingsley Publishers
London and Philadelphia

First published in 2008
by Jessica Kingsley Publishers
116 Pentonville Road
London N1 9JB, UK
and
400 Market Street, Suite 400
Philadelphia, PA 19106, USA

www.jkp.com

Library of Congress Cataloging in Publication Data
Holzhauser-Peters, Leslie.
   Making sense of children's thinking and behavior : a step-by-step tool for understanding children with NLD, Asperger's, HFA, PDD-NOS, and other neurological differences / Leslie Holzhauser-Peters and Leslie True.
      p. cm.
   Includes index.
   ISBN 978-1-84310-888-7 (pb : alk. paper) 1. Cognition disorders in children. 2. Cognition in children--Testing. 3. Children with mental disabilities--Psychology. I. True, Leslie. II. Title.
   RJ506.C63H65 2008
   618.92'8--dc22

                                        2008002665

British Library Cataloguing in Publication Data
A CIP catalogue record for this book is available from the British Library

ISBN 978 1 84310 888 7

Printed and bound in Great Britain by
Athenaeum Press, Gateshead, Tyne and Wear

This book is dedicated to Joshua.
Thank you for teaching and helping us
to understand how the world looks through your
eyes. Thank you for allowing us to share your life
with others in the hope of making life better
for those that come after you. You give new
meaning to the word "courage"
as you face the world each day.
We love you.

Contents

About the Authors

Leslie True holds a Bachelor's degree in Business Administration from Bowling Green State University. She is the mother of three sons—Joshua, Danny, and Michael. Her oldest son, Joshua, has been diagnosed with a nonverbal learning disability (NLD). For the past year Leslie has worked as an instructional aide for a child diagnosed with a nonverbal learning disability. As a parent, she has done extensive studying and reading in the field of NLD. Her greatest qualification here is that she is an informed, intelligent, caring mother of a child diagnosed with NLD.

Leslie Holzhauser-Peters holds a Bachelor's degree from the University of Cincinnati and a Master's degree from Miami University. She has thirty years of experience working in the public school setting in the special education and general education fields. She has worked as a speech–language pathologist, supervisor, and curriculum consultant. Her areas of expertise are language, literacy, and intervention. She has provided service to children diagnosed with NLD and has done extensive study in the areas of NLD and Asperger's. In addition she has presented throughout the United States and has authored several publications. Over the past several years she has acted both as an advocate and speech–language pathologist to her co-author's son, Joshua.

How the authors met

All it takes is one person to believe. Dianne Clemens was that special person for Joshua. She listened and always helped to figure out ways to make his life better. When everyone continued to insist Joshua was fine, she never dismissed the concerns that were ever present. Aside from being an outstanding speech–language pathologist, Dianne is a wonderful, caring person with a big heart and a never-ending willingness to help. Dianne worked with Joshua professionally early on and continues to this day to be a significant source of support and guidance.

The authors met because Dianne introduced them to one another in the hope that Leslie Holzhauser-Peters could provide speech–language pathology and advocacy services to Joshua, prior to his diagnosis. Dianne and Leslie H-P had previously worked together as speech–language pathologists, and became friends as they worked tirelessly to help children over the years. Knowing Dianne's love for children and having great respect for her work, Leslie H-P agreed to Dianne's appeal to consult on Joshua's case.

Leslie H-P did provide speech–language services in Joshua's home, and she and Leslie True became great friends over the course of the many discussions that arose surrounding Joshua's communication and related issues. The two of them have endured many hardships together, as there were great difficulties in getting Joshua diagnosed and on an IEP (Individual Education Plan) at school. He looked too good, and no one would believe the concerns the two Leslies expressed. Needless to say, the struggles have been many and intense, but they have been bearable because the two Leslies had each other. These two women feel blessed that out of such pain they both found a lifelong friend.

Authors' notes on the stories in this book

The stories in this book describe real situations that are encountered by children diagnosed with neurological impairments, and are intended to illustrate to parents and professionals the kind of situations they might encounter, in the hope that they will then better understand the thinking of these children. The thinking tool provided can be used with children with nonverbal learning disability (NLD), Asperger's, high-functioning autism, pervasive developmental disorder-not otherwise specified (PDD-NOS), and other neurological disorders. Many of the stories are told from the first-person perspective, as they are about Leslie True's son Joshua. He is currently twelve years old and in the seventh grade—however, the stories are taken from different points in his life. Others are a synthesis of stories based on a variety of children with neurological disorders that we have worked with and discussed. In order to distinguish between the two and make those stories more reader-friendly, we have chosen to use the name Grace when referring to these children throughout the book.

NLD

I don't know much about NLD. But what I do know is I have sensitive hearing, I don't know my own strength, I have a good memory, and I have piano talents. I want to know more about it. I wish someone could teach me more about NLD. I have my mom call. It's better if I know more. It could help me understand it. It's the only way for me to understand it all. I sometimes wish I didn't have NLd then things would be so much better. I want to know about what will NLD be like when I'm an adult. I also want to know if I'm going to be better when I'm much older. I'd like it if somebody told me about all this.

Introduction

Living with a child with a neurological difference like nonverbal learning disability (NLD), Asperger's, high-functioning autism, and pervasive developmental disorder-not otherwise specified (PDD-NOS) is devastating. It impacts every
aspect of their life, everyone they encounter at every event they attend. It's difficult to explain, it's difficult to see, and as a result is even more difficult to believe.
To constantly attempt to explain to everyone you encounter is exhausting. On a
daily basis, the family has to deal with the repercussions these differences
present. Add this to having to deal with everyone else's perceptions and misconceptions, and it can seem to be an insurmountable task. As you attempt to
protect your child, you constantly encounter the scrutiny of everyone around
you. You're considered a bad parent because you don't discipline, you're over-
protective, you're not fostering their independence, or you're just plain crazy. As
a parent, you are willing to subject yourself to the constant review of people
who think they know more about what's best for your child than you.

The common misconception about children with a neurological difference
revolves around the notion that what works for neurotypical children will surely
work for them too, because they look so normal. The flaw in that way of
thinking is that you fail to look at the world through their eyes. Everyone
responds to children in a "one size fits all" manner unless there is a visible
handicap, in which case appropriate accommodations are usually willingly
made. With neurological differences, the child's view of the world is not typical,
and therefore requires appropriate accommodations unique to their needs.
Sadly, it's incredibly difficult to get the accommodations they need to survive.

Think, why would a parent be willing to subject himself or herself to repeated criticism, unless they absolutely believed it was necessary for their child's survival?

When you understand neurological differences and you are able to see the world through the child's eyes, the world looks quite scary, due to the uncertainty they experience in everything they do. Once you begin to realize their perspective, you start to understand the stress, anxiety, and general emotional devastation they can regularly experience. As a parent, when you understand this, you are willing to endure any amount of criticism in order to get the help the child needs. The world for them is full of constant obstacles to overcome. Every action that they take is pursued with an uncertain outcome. They go through their day as if in a minefield, never knowing where or when the explosion will occur. They wouldn't choose to step on the mine if they knew it was there, but they don't. Their differences keep them from knowing. Can you imagine waking up knowing you have to go through your day never being sure if your next action will cause someone to be angry or unhappy with you? The fear generated from this is ever present and is the best state the child can hope for. Their anxiety levels continue to be compounded, based on the way they are perceived and consequently treated. Now imagine being a ten-year-old living with that nightmare every day. It's never gone. It's our belief that the only way to improve the quality of the child's life is to see the world through their eyes in order to help them maneuver through the minefield.

The purpose in writing this book is to help those who work with and love children diagnosed with neurological differences to develop a systematic way to analyze their thinking and behavior. Children diagnosed as such are misunderstood and often give an illusion of competence. They appear so totally competent in some areas that people have difficulty believing they are not competent in all areas. Those of us who love these children know that is not the case. They look too good. They make decisions based on their perception of the world. Even though their perceptions are so different from everyone else's, it is their reality and the basis that they use for moving forward and making decisions. It is often hard to believe, much less understand, why they do what they do. However, understanding is the key to helping them have a successful life. Figuring out their initial understanding of a situation helps to explain the choices and actions they make. Once you are better able to decipher their thinking, you gain the insight that enables you to assess the situation in a reasonable, calm manner. Often the things these children do appear to be intentional. They appear to be choosing to be defiant, manipulative, or disrespectful.

The best-case scenario is, their behavior appears to be odd. In the worst-case scenario, the behavior looks like it should be punished.

The better you understand how it must be to live with a neurological difference, the better equipped you'll be to make meaningful changes to improve these children's quality of life. This makes it necessary to have a system in place to provide an alternative to punishment. Punishment has no impact on changing their behavior and only serves to erode their already diminished self-esteem. There needs to be a way to systematically think through why they do what they do. It is essential that those who live and work around them develop an ability to thoroughly analyze the situation and the actions taken by the child. With an analytical system in place, parents and professionals can go from a mindset of frustration and punishment to one of determining why the behavior is happening, and what steps can be taken to fix it. It is hoped this book will be used to help families and professionals see the world through the eyes of these children. When you develop the ability to see what they see, the magnitude of what they deal with on a daily basis appears overwhelming and causes you to feel great empathy.

For these children, the biggest obstacle to overcome is the inability of those around them to believe the extent of their differences. It's difficult to convince people, but not impossible. Those who do come to believe, typically have an "aha" moment. The "aha" moment is when they suddenly see it and begin to attempt to understand. It is only then that they start to believe. Once the "aha" moment occurs, they are more willing to help the child. It is critical that people involved in the lives of these children reach their "aha" moment. It has been our experience that using a systematic approach helps people reach the necessary level of understanding, and so we have created a thinking tool for families and professionals to use to facilitate that process.

Unfortunately, both of us have had to learn first-hand, with limited support and guidance, how to cope. This book and tool are our attempt to make the lives of those who read it a little bit better. We felt that sharing the real-life experiences of the children in our lives afflicted with neurological differences might serve a twofold purpose. First, we hope readers can identify with the stories and gain some comfort in knowing they are not alone. Second, we wanted to provide families and professionals with a tool that we found to be successful, and which we hope will help to improve the quality of the lives of those affected. Throughout this book we will draw from the real-life stories involving the children we live with, work with, and discuss. Children diagnosed with neurological differences exhibit their strengths and weaknesses in different areas.

We acknowledge that no two children are alike. However, the thinking tool presented here has the ability to address problem areas of children at all developmental levels.

Throughout our journey, we have found that people are on a continuum in terms of their thinking and willingness to believe. Fortunately, along the way, there have been "aha" moments for the people involved in Joshua's life. Before the start of school, as is typical, we meet the educational team Joshua will be working with. One particular year, we provided the team with scenarios of behavior that had occurred during the previous year. After using the thinking tool, we were able to submit the scenarios along with explanations of what Joshua might have been thinking, resulting in his actions. Within the first week of school this proved beneficial, as a teacher stopped me to tell me what had happened during class. She was passing out cookies to practice manners. After handing Joshua a cookie, she said, "What do you say?" He replied, with a huge grin, "My mom makes really good cookies." She repeated, "No, what do you say after I give you a cookie?" Josh repeated, "My mom makes really good cookies." The children next to him reminded him to say "thank you." Owing to her *implied* request, Joshua didn't understand what she expected of him. Having the scenarios we shared fresh in her mind, she was willing to listen, look, and believe. This allowed her to recognize Joshua's conduct as a result of his differences, when she could easily have considered it rude and intentional. This was her "aha" moment. After this, she was able to play a very important role in helping Joshua to have a good year.

Another "seeing is believing" example of an "aha" moment involves the counselor at school. Joshua liked the school counselor. It was a safe place for him to be. He knew he would not be teased, bullied, or blamed. For three years, Joshua saw the counselor by himself. The counselor always listened to what I had to say about Joshua. He never acted like he didn't believe me, but he never seemed to totally understand where I was coming from—until one day when the light bulb came on, his "aha" moment. He had started seeing Joshua with a small group of other children. It happened to be Joshua's birthday, so everyone sang to him, substituting in the words "You look like a monkey and smell like one too," as children sometimes do. Instead of the typical child's reaction, a shy smile, slightly embarrassed, Joshua immediately put his hands over his ears and assumed what I call the "cocoon position" where he tries to block out the outside world. He didn't realize the other children were joking by singing the song that way. He thought they were intentionally being cruel to him. From that moment on, the counselor seemed to have reached a new level of understanding. All of a sudden it was possible for him to believe that the behaviors I had been describing might actually be happening—and that maybe, just maybe, there was more to this boy who looked so normal.

This book includes a thinking tool that provides a way to decode the actions of a child with neurological differences. This system is specifically designed to be used with children diagnosed with NLD, Asperger's, high-functioning autism, and PDD-NOS. Each chapter addresses a different problem area for these children, with real-life examples of behavior and actions related to that problem area. Included are many examples of the types of behaviors encountered when living with or educating the child, along with examples of how to use the thinking tool to plan effectively for the child.

In summary, this book provides a systematic way to think about and analyze the actions of children with neurological differences in order to see the world as they see it in the attempt to help them. By using this systematic decoding process, we hope that good decisions for the neurologically different child, as well as those around them, can be made. As the thinking system is practiced and used over and over, it becomes internalized and automatic, so that appropriate decisions about how to react to a situation or specific behavior are more easily made. For your convenience, summary and full versions of the Systematic Tool to Analyze Thinking (STAT) can be found in Appendices I and II.

Chapter 1

The Systematic Tool
to Analyze Thinking (STAT)

The Systematic Tool to Analyze Thinking (STAT) came into being as a result of hours of discussion focused on Joshua and Grace's actions and reactions to different situations that arose throughout the course of the day. We would discuss why *we thought* they did what they did. Eventually we discovered you have to look at a situation through their eyes and think about how they might perceive it. Anyone who has parented a neurotypical child realizes that what you instinctively do with them is not effective when dealing with a child with neurological differences. Almost always, the path you need to take with these children is counter-intuitive. *Therefore, you must resist the urge to respond the way you normally would with any other child.*

Our discussions led to countless hours of analyzing the outcome of situations and why they might have occurred. After doing this for a period of over two years, we realized we had developed a systematic way to hypothesize about Joshua and Grace's thinking and reacting. The purpose of the STAT is to try and determine the child's perceptions of the world around them—the ultimate goal being, once you can perceive the world as they do, to understand their thought process, pinpoint the problem, and then develop a plan of action. Oftentimes, the knee-jerk response to their behavior assumes that the child has made a mean-spirited choice. Once you analyze their actions, it's usually clear that they respond in a manner that is not a choice but a direct result of their neurological differences.

For instance, one day when Joshua was eight years old, he and his brother Michael had been playing video games in the basement. Suddenly, Michael came running up the steps, crying. "What's wrong?" I asked. "Joshua smacked me on the side of my head!" Naturally, I called Joshua up to explain. "What?" he said, truly oblivious to why I had called him. "Why did you smack Michael in the head?" "He kept screwing up the game!" he said in his *the answer is so obvious* tone. "So you hit him in the head?" "Yeah, I was trying to knock some sense into him." From his tone of voice it was quite clear he was very serious and totally believed this to be possible. Whenever someone hits, you automatically assume they did so with malicious intent. At first glance, this appeared to be the situation here. Without further investigation, I never would have known what Joshua was thinking or that he did what he did for any other reason than to be mean. However, because of his inability to understand figurative language, hitting Michael was Joshua's honest attempt to fix the problem.

If this situation had happened between two neurotypical children, then, assuming the intent was to be mean, a punishment intended to result in a behavior change would be given. This conventional reaction to the neurotypical child is a justified negative reaction, which one hopes will achieve the desired outcome of changing behavior. However, in Joshua's case, there was no negative intent, therefore a punishment would not be understood and wouldn't result in any improvement or long-term behavioral change.

Simply put, the STAT can be used by anyone desiring to improve the quality of life of the child. It has been our experience that when one person in the family is able to use this tool, others quickly learn. For instance, once a parent understands this system and discusses everyday scenarios with grandparents and other family members, they too begin to use it independently.

For example, when Joshua was eleven, his grandpa had set up a weekly time for Joshua and a boy from school to play golf. Both boys were new to the sport, so we felt it would be a good opportunity for some social interaction for Joshua. After returning one afternoon, my dad said he noticed that Joshua was incessantly talking and not giving the other boy a chance to speak or otherwise comment. He remarked that Joshua appeared uneasy. He felt the talking was the way his nervousness was manifesting itself. He wasn't sure of the source of this feeling but had made a guess as to the possibilities. He felt Joshua could have been anxious because playing golf was a new experience; or he was nervous about being with another kid; or both. Without really realizing, my dad had gone through the STAT process. He was able to do this simply as a result of listening to me break down other situations as I tried to get to the core of Joshua's thinking. He listened, he was willing, and he believed, and therefore he was able to actively participate in making Joshua's life better.

It is also extremely beneficial to use the STAT when trying to explain the child's thinking to the educational staff who will be working with the child. Many different people will come in contact with your child. Obviously anyone who is in constant contact with your child in the educational setting could benefit from being introduced to this tool. These individuals might be general and special education teachers, including substitutes, instructional aides, speech–language pathologists, psychologists, counselors, teachers of physical education, art, and music as well as occupational and physical therapists. Parents need to consider informing other school staff members who may interact with their child. These individuals might include school administrators, bus drivers, cafeteria workers, playground aides, and maintenance staff. As parents of children with neurological differences know, circumstances that require explanation occur on a regular basis. Parents will not be able to be in contact with all of the school personnel mentioned here, which is why it is essential that there is a core group of people who have an ability to identify behaviors caused by the neurological differences. In difficult circumstances the STAT allows parents to take what is considered bizarre behavior and provide a meaningful explanation as to why it may have occurred.

Consider this unusual example. I received a phone call from the assistant principal of Joshua's school during his fourth grade year. She told me a maintenance person from the school was in the bathroom and heard someone urinating on the floor. When Joshua came out, the maintenance person took him to the assistant principal's office. When she asked Joshua why he was doing that, he said he didn't feel comfortable using the urinals. After telling me about the bathroom incident she asked me why I thought this had happened. At this point, I was at a loss and could think of no reasonable explanation for Joshua's behavior. I did know three things, though. First, this wasn't a normal pattern of behavior. Second, I didn't have enough information to even begin to make a guess. Third, there was a reason, albeit logical in his mind only. Hence, the perfect situation in which to use the STAT. More on the outcome of this story later.

You might not think it imperative to inform all other school personnel, but after speaking with, for instance, bus drivers, I found they would prefer to know. One driver told me "It would be helpful to know, just like you would tell a teacher, because it would make it easier to cope with situations that might come up."

Parents oftentimes encounter situations where their child's behavior needs to be interpreted, so that the individuals involved gain an understanding of what has occurred. If you get lucky enough to encounter a parent who is kind enough to ask about your child's unusual behavior, it gives you a chance to provide a reasonable explanation. This enables the parent of the same-age peer to go back and explain to her child what occurred and why, thus fostering a continued friendship and a tolerant and safe environment to visit. Your child is thus given the opportunity to function as close to normal as possible, thanks to the reduction of anxiety.

We, as a family, have been blessed to have in our lives just this type of relationship. Joshua has had a friendship with Nick since they were four. The benefits of a relationship that started so young have turned out to be numerous. Because Nick has spent so much time with Joshua, he is much more tolerant of his "quirks," writing them off most times as "that's just Josh." Also, Nick's family has witnessed the journey we've been on with Joshua's nonverbal learning disability (NLD), so they are extremely compassionate and willing to help in any way they can. They continue to provide Joshua a safe place where he can try and have those genuine moments of friendship so rare for NLDer's.

One afternoon, Nick's mom, Jane, was bringing the boys back from the pool. They were ten at the time. She described what appeared to be Joshua's attempt to strike up a casual conversation with Nick. Joshua said, "So, Nick, have you heard about Insight?" Nick replied that he had not. Continuing, Joshua said, as if he was reading an ad, "It's a natural male enhancement drug." Obviously, this immediately got Jane's attention. Adjusting the rearview mirror, she said, "Where did you hear that?" "I saw it on TV." Fortunately, the conversation ended there. When they got home, Jane shared the details with me. You would think that after being faced with a number of these bizarre episodes, you would become immune to the shock, but I always seem to be just as surprised each and every time. I told Jane there was no way Joshua knew what that meant. That is, in fact, what happened. After having identified where on TV he saw this particular product, he confirmed he did not know what it was for. When I went on to explain, he was quite surprised, saying, "That's disgusting!"

Because Jane has always been willing to listen and believe, I was able to explain that, Joshua was just repeating what he had heard without any comprehension, commonly referred to as echolalia and very typical of children with NLD. As a result, she didn't go away thinking Joshua was a bad kid trying to corrupt Nick. Fortunately the whole conversation didn't have much impact on Nick. Jane said he never asked about it later. She thinks he just chalked it up as one of many times Joshua talks "over his head." Most helpful, though, was the fact that I was able to clear this up at home by explaining it to Joshua before he went to, say, school, and had the same conversation with the principal, perhaps, where the tolerance level would certainly not be so high. It enabled me to head off a potentially explosive situation before it became a major issue. We are extremely blessed to have a family like Nick's, who accepts Joshua for who he is and tries to understand him by having a constant open line of communication. It is a rare and priceless gift.

As has been illustrated, children diagnosed with neurological differences spend a disproportionate amount of time being blamed for actions that were not intended to be negative. The STAT (see Appendix I) is intended to be a system that provides its users with a method for looking at the behavior of the child and analyzing it, resulting in the ability to react to it in a positive way. After repeated use you will find the application of this system becomes automatic because you have internalized the process. We truly believe that using this approach will improve the life of those affected by these types of neurological differences.

How to use the Systematic Tool to Analyze Thinking (STAT)

As previously mentioned, we think that people interested in understanding children with neurological differences have an "aha" moment that enables them to change their perception of the child's behavior and begin to work more effectively towards improving the child's quality of life.

Step 1: Assess the situation

• **Describe the situation you want to analyze**
• **Determine what you know**
  ◦ Who was there?
  ◦ What was said?
  ◦ What actions were taken?
  ◦ Where did it happen?
  ◦ When did it happen?
  ◦ The physical and emotional state of the person—tired, emotionally vulnerable, etc.?
• **Ask questions of your child or others if more information is needed**
  ◦ Why did you do that?
  ◦ Tell me exactly what happened?
  ◦ What happened first, next, then?

The focus of Step 1 is to describe the situation in some detail. As you use the STAT, you will find that some situations allow you to determine what your child was thinking, while others will be more difficult. There will be many situations where you are present, and these may or may not require an additional question or two. The more difficult the situation is to figure out, the more information you need. Oftentimes the answers may lie in what may be considered inconsequential at the out set. As illustrated in the bathroom incident (known from here on out as the "great bathroom caper"), initially, the assistant principal presented her view of what had occurred and I didn't have enough information to develop a hypothesis. Once I got more information, I was able to determine what had happened and why.

This first step is critical because without the correct information you will probably embark on a journey down the wrong path. The wrong information here will lead to making an incorrect choice about actions to be considered later. It's that old idea of "garbage in, garbage out." Parents know that you cannot usually rely on one source to get the correct description of the situation. Oftentimes for the most difficult situations, pieces of a puzzle need to be put together by talking to your child and others who might have been involved or witnessed it. As with anything else, everyone comes with his or her own perspective. As we know, children with neurological differences often misinterpret situations, but it is also clear that others can misinterpret their actions in a situation as well. These misinterpretations make it critical, especially in the more serious situations, to get as clear a picture as possible of what actually occurred.

In the "great bathroom caper," the assistant principal might have thought Joshua was being disrespectful and an all around bad kid. However, going through Joshua's actions step by step, I determined that he had waited until the last possible moment to go and had little time to assess his options. He felt uncomfortable using the urinals due to the lack of privacy, so he went to the stalls. Stall one had urine on the floor and seat. Stall two was filled with multiple waste and Joshua didn't want to go on top of it. When I asked him why he didn't flush the toilet he said he thought the handle would be dirty. He simply ran out of time and viable options. After all this questioning about his actions and thoughts surrounding them, the situation was so much more clear to me. I finally could continue on in the process of developing a hypothesis with a complete picture of the details.

Once you feel you have enough information, then move to Step 2 to develop a hypothesis to determine *why* the child did what they did and what they might have been thinking. It is in this step that you try to see the world through their eyes.

Step 2: Develop a hypothesis

The STAT incorporates twelve choices. Each choice describes one of the major deficit areas noted in these children. This tool includes a brief description of the characteristics of that particular deficit area. Within each box, most of the examples given refer to specific areas of difficulty experienced by these children; however, a few examples are used to describe needs or how a child may appear and are so noted. Each of these areas will be discussed and described separately in the following chapters. As you think through your child's actions and scenarios, you will find one or more of the areas may be identified in trying to determine a cause. When developing the hypothesis, there will often be one obvious choice. At this point you may be able to make a guess as to what your child may be saying to himself. The purpose of this section is to try and think in the way your child might be thinking. For example, when Joshua tried to knock some sense into Michael, our two-minute conversation was enough for me to realize Joshua's misunderstanding of an idiom was the cause of the problem.

In other situations, two or more deficit areas may be selected because they have each played a part in causing the child to see the situation as they do and determined their reaction to it. Such was the case one Christmas morning when Joshua was ten. He was literally bouncing from wall to wall, running up and down the hallway. As I watched his actions, I was able to assess the situation and develop this hypothesis: *with all of the anticipation of opening presents, he doesn't know what to do with all the emotion.* Emotion was the deficit area that was at the root of his actions. The second deficit area affected was the sensory, i.e. the input that he needed to receive from bouncing off the walls—his reaction to, or way of dealing with, the cause. He needed some release for that pent-up emotion and needed to get it out.

As you continue your journey and learn more about your child's neurological differences, you begin to realize how many deficit areas there can be and how far-reaching the effects can be in every aspect of their life. The more you know, the more overwhelming it seems. The beauty of this phase of the STAT is that it clearly lays out, in a systematic way, choices that help to clarify your thinking.

At this point in the process, you have developed a guess about what your child might have been thinking. You have looked at the situation through their

Step 2: Developing a hypothesis

Why? Why did they react the way they did? What could they be thinking? Select one or more of the elements below.

Abstract language
- Literal thinking
- Figurative language/jokes, humor
- Implied/inferential
- Rhetorical questions/sarcasm
- Idioms/compound words
- Multiple meaning words
- Vocabulary
- Character development words (respect, honesty, responsibility)
- Directions/assignments

Control/consistency
- Difficulty transitioning and adapting to change
- Need to control situation so will know what will happen
- Need to rely on rules and routines
- Need schedule for predictability and to feel safe
- Often have area of specialist interest
- Appear rigid, directive, bossy

Mental flexibility
- Abstract vs concrete concepts
- Big picture vs focus on detail
- Focus on unimportant vs significant
- Ability to generalize or transfer skill
- Main ideas and summaries
- Cause and effect
- Understanding consequences of actions
- Prioritizing
- Editing/redoing
- Are inflexible/one right way
- Seem rude/correcting others
- Appear perfectionistic/bossy
- Thinking logical/fact oriented
- Learn by explanation and doing

Motor
- Handwriting
- Dressing (zipping, buttoning, tying shoes)
- Art (coloring, cutting)
- Eating (cutting, spilling)
- Walking, running, skipping
- Catching, throwing
- Riding a bike
- Balance/safety issues (curbs, uneven surfaces, playing equip)

Thinking about others thinking
- Theory of mind
- Perspective taking
- Empathy
- Encourage
- Consoling
- Apologizing
- Complimenting
- Compromising/negotiating
- Sharing
- Offering or asking for help
- Persuading
- Imagining or pretending
- Detecting deception (gullible)
- Understanding motive or intent
- Manners
- Explaining
- Using mental state verbs (think, know, believe)
- Understanding author's purpose/point of view
- Mood/theme
- Audience and purpose
- Forming friendships/relationships
- Working as part of group
- Are mindblind
- Are not embarrassed
- Don't lie or steal
- Don't deceive
- Are brutally honest (tell fat, bald)

Impulsivity
- Blurting out/act before think
- Consequences of actions
- Rushing through
- Waiting
- Deeper thinking
- Anticipation
- Stopping
- Excessive, exaggerated reactions

Sensory
- Sounds/tastes and textures/smells
- Touch (slapping, hugging)
- Pressure (slamming, squeezing)
- Pain tolerance/sensitivity (hypo/hyper)
- Hygiene/clothing
- Staring/eye contact
- Busy, noisy environments
- Overload

Social communication
- What to say/who to say it to
- Where, when, how to say it
- Initiate, maintain, end conversation
- Monitor understanding, repair and adjust
- Limited conversational turns/monologue
- Reading or using social cues
- Facial expressions, body language, tone
- Explain/small talk
- Speaks same way to adults as peers
- Questions (too many, too few, personal)
- Echolalia
- Friendship/dating/relationships

Executive functions
- Identify a problem
- Problem solve
- Plan
- Sequence
- Organize
- Prioritize
- Complex tasks
- Multi-step directions
- Projects
- No sense of time

Spatial orientation
- Body in space (bump into people and things, trip)
- Finding locations (lost, disoriented, late)
- Navigating environments
- Manipulating objects (pouring, placement)
- Uncoordinated/clumsy
- Maps and graphs
- Lining up numbers
- Staying in the margins
- Visually busy worksheets
- Copying from board, paper

Emotions
- Identify feelings of self or others
- Expressing own feelings
- Emotional reciprocity
- Over/understated emotional reaction
- Gradients of emotions (agitated to furious)
- Emotional intelligence
- Understanding one person can have many feelings, same event
- Understanding two people can have different emotions, same event
- Friendships/relationships
- Mood in text/inferential emotions in text
- Often look happy but not

Anxiety
- Suicide/depression
- Meltdowns/shut down
- Exhaustion/stress/fear/target for bullies
- Need for downtime/solitary time
- Need breaks
- Need reassurance, use check phrases (I'm okay?)
- Need social circles of acceptance
- Need safe interactions
- Anxiety indicators (vomiting, self-talk, twirling)

Hypothesis about their thinking (take a guess)—What could they be thinking to themselves? What would they be saying?

eyes. In many situations, you will feel you've made a definitive and correct choice and move straight on to Step 4 with a good deal of certainty. However, this may not always be the case. Our experience has been that some circumstances are complicated, and at this point you may not feel completely confident that you have correctly identified the source of the problem. You simply cannot determine how your child was thinking. If you are saying to yourself, "It could be this, it could be that, but I'm really not sure," or "I have no idea why this happened," then you need to move to Step 3, which involves asking more specific questions. This is an information gathering phase, but it may come to you in pieces and occur over time.

Step 3 (optional): Ask questions to obtain a step-by-step account

Types of questions
- Ask literal questions to try to prove your hypothesis.
- Ask questions that have a black-and-white answer.
- Ask questions that require a one- or two-word response.
- Provide answer choices to make it more concrete.
- Ask questions that address social cues such as body language (i.e. What did the person do that made you think that? What was she doing with her hands? etc.).

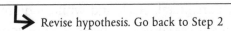 Revise hypothesis. Go back to Step 2

On one occasion in fifth grade, Joshua's teacher emailed me to let me know of a situation that had occurred that day. She had blown a whistle to show the students what it would signal in a game. Joshua started whistling feeling very proud he could whistle through his teeth. After many students laughed, he persisted after a normal quieting down time until two girls repeatedly asked him to stop, growing increasingly agitated when he wouldn't. After a lengthy discussion with Leslie H-P, we decided it was a social communication problem, but we needed more information to figure out which direction to take. For instance, why were the girls telling Joshua to stop? Were they being nice, trying to keep him out of trouble? Were they puzzled as to why he continued to whistle? Or, were they aggravated by the disruption? Also, we needed to have an indication of what their nonverbal cues were, how their faces looked, their bodies, and their tone of voice. What did the teacher say and how? After a follow up email, his teacher explained that Josh did not understand that she was ready to continue, and that therefore, he should be quiet. The girls seemed agitated that he didn't get the teacher's cue when she said, "OK…OK." They first looked at him impatiently, then at the same time said, "Shhh! Stop, Josh." The teacher reported that after that direct signal he did stop, but didn't appear to realize he had done anything out of the norm. Once we received the specific details, we could go back to Step 2 and develop a more specific hypothesis—that being, that because Joshua is usually not well received socially by his peers, it's possible he continued longer than is appropriate to sustain this positive peer interaction. Now that we thought we had pinpointed what he was thinking, we were better prepared to continue on with the steps of the STAT and develop a plan that could enable us to use this as a teachable moment.

It is at this point that you are asking very specific questions. You want a very detailed step-by-step description of what occurred. You want enough information to be able to picture it in your mind as it occurred, including direct quotes, facial expressions, hand gestures, and tone of voice. In the above example, asking the teacher for the details in an email was advantageous for a couple of reasons. First, it resulted in her having to relay the experience in a detailed sequential manner, providing details that could be missed in an oral conversation. Second, it was a written account of the situation that can be analyzed, reviewed, and revisited as often as necessary to move you to making that definitive hypothesis. When addressing your child, again, you need to ask questions that are literal, black-and-white, require a one- or two-word response, providing answer choices to make it more concrete where necessary. It is also important to be sure to ask, in a very specific way, questions concerning the body language and social cues of the people involved. For example, "Where were her hands? What did she do? What did you do? Was she looking at you?" As you know, your child may often need to be guided through this process and given wait time as needed. It can take a lot of time to get a little information. Once you've got your questions answered and have gathered more information, go back to Step 2 to confirm or revise your hypothesis.

Finally, you have reached the point of choosing what actions to consider. We hope that once you've been able to see the situation through the child's eyes, you will have a clearer understanding about what you should do. The STAT provides five actions to consider.

There are times when you might not want to take any action. Think again about the scenario of Joshua literally bouncing off the walls on Christmas morning. I made the decision not to do anything because I felt he needed the sensory input to deal with the overwhelming emotion he was feeling.

Many situations will lead you to provide a detailed, logical explanation to your child. It is often surprising what needs to be explained and the depth to

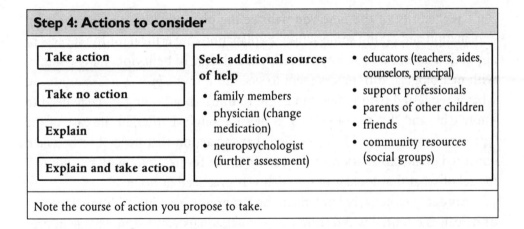

Step 4: Actions to consider		

Take action	**Seek additional sources of help**	• educators (teachers, aides, counselors, principal)
Take no action	• family members	• support professionals
Explain	• physician (change medication)	• parents of other children
		• friends
Explain and take action	• neuropsychologist (further assessment)	• community resources (social groups)

Note the course of action you propose to take.

which you must do so. Using this system will help you identify what needs to be explained and to what extent.

Most parents would be surprised to have to explain when and why you say "thank you" because it is a skill neurotypical children pick up intuitively. In our case, it does require an explanation. Last year, Joshua's dad, Todd, made a display case for Joshua's cherished monster truck collection. After many hours of work and surely excited about the reaction he hoped to get, Todd brought the completed product up to show Joshua. Joshua looked at it and said, "Looks good." Danny, Joshua's younger brother, said, "Joshua, aren't you going to say 'thank you'?" Joshua said very seriously, "I need to see if it's going to work first." He didn't recognize the time and effort that had been taken on his behalf. In his mind, "If it doesn't work, I won't be appreciative, so I won't need to say 'thank you'." He needed a detailed explanation as to why it was necessary to say "thank you" at that time.

Sometimes you may simply choose to take action without providing an explanation. These situations revolve around actions that require changing the environment or the surrounding circumstances of an everyday event. Often-times parents structure the environment in a way that allows for less upset to the household. For example, in our house, there are two sinks in the bathroom that our three sons, Joshua, Danny, and Michael, were expected to share. After repeated conflicts over a variety of different things, I felt it would be better to remove Joshua from the situation. It seemed as if it was too much for him to have to deal with while trying to manage his nightly routine. I told him he could move his toiletries to our bathroom and start to use it on a regular basis. He was fine with that and peace soon followed, at least in that one area.

The majority of the time you will see the plan of action requires both an explanation and taking some action. Explanations are critical for the success of any action taken that you hope to result in a change of behavior. Many children with neurological differences seem to need to know *why* it is necessary to do what is requested before they can begin to think about doing it. They need to know why, and "because I said so" is never enough. Earlier, in the case of the "great bathroom caper," I determined that the action that needed to be taken consisted of an explanation of what to do in the future along with providing a model of what that looked like, which was practiced at home.

In order to effectively implement the last option, seeking additional sources of help, it is essential you research any professionals you might engage in providing support. Finding the right professional includes researching their knowledge base and experience regarding your child's particular situation. You want to make sure the service obtained is effective and meaningful. The support you seek does not always have to be from paid professionals, but can incorporate family, friends, and services that are available in your community.

We've outlined a way to use this system that has been successful for us, but it is our hope you will use it in any way you think will benefit you and your child.

Chapter 2

Abstract Language

A line from a book: "You didn't have to bite my head off."

Joshua's response: "Ooh, gross!"

There the teacher stood in the classroom, obviously irritated, after telling Grace to pay attention for the second time. Approaching Grace, she firmly asked, "What part of 'pay attention' did you not understand?" Her reply: "All of it." Taking it as an obvious lack of respect, the teacher immediately sent Grace to the principal's office. In her own reality, Grace truly just answered the question asked, not understanding the implied meaning of "do what you are told."

The language of children diagnosed as having neurological differences is yet another aspect of their life that works both for them and against them. As in so many other areas of their life, they look too good, so no one believes there is a problem. As you speak with them they seem so articulate and bright, maybe even gifted. As an adult, when you talk with them you feel sure they understand. They typically engage adults in conversations about a topic that shows their extensive knowledge. Adults usually adjust the conversation to make the communication event a successful one. Because the conversation seems so normal and because the children have no visible disability, it's almost impossible to believe they have difficulty responding to simple commands or language that much younger children understand.

The area of language transcends many aspects of everyday life. In the life of these children, language is an area that causes numerous misunderstandings that result in negative consequences for them. Unfortunately because of their language deficits, they are often punished and really don't have any clue as to why. Language is such a broad-based and pervasive area, and we have chosen to focus on abstract language. We've chosen to look at what the child misunderstands, as well as the problems that arise when their communication partner misunderstands due to abstract language.

In reality, these children have a very concrete and literal understanding of what is discussed. This causes the child to look defiant or manipulative when they truly don't understand. So much of our language is abstract; therefore, much of what is said around them is misunderstood. Abstract language appears in various forms throughout our day. Once you begin to notice how much abstract language surrounds us, you begin to realize how difficult and overwhelming it must be for children who are such literal thinkers.

Think for a moment about how many rhetorical questions children are asked in an effort to change or correct their behavior. Questions like, What are you supposed to be doing? Did you forget something? Where should you be now? are often asked at home and school to notify them that they are not engaged in the required activity. The child responds in a very literal way by answering the question as a question, not realizing that it was a directive. This often makes them appear to be defiant when they truly believe they have answered the question as the person intended. For example, the question Did you forget something? could typically be answered with a simple no. In their minds, if they knew they forgot something, they already would have gotten it. Similarly, if they knew what they were supposed to be doing, they would be doing it, and if they knew where they were supposed to be, they would be there. These types of rhetorical questions make no sense to them.

A perfect example happened one evening when Joshua was in the bathroom after taking a shower. He called me in, sounding very proud of whatever it was he was about to show me. "Look," he said, "I cut my hair." Horrified at the sight before me, I exclaimed, "Why did you cut your hair!" "Because it was in my eyes," he said, sadly, seeing my obvious dismay. Clearly, what I really meant was, "Oh my gosh, what have you done!" However, he answered my question as if it was just that. To him, there was a problem. His hair was in his eyes and bothering him. Under different circumstances, I would be proud of him for problem-solving the situation on his own. In this instance, I would definitely have preferred him running it by me before he took action. Monumental as it seemed in the moment, and disheartened as he was to find out he hadn't done a good thing, in the end, a quick emergency trip to the barber returned us to our version of a normal life. I am sure this particular example has been played out many times in numerous typical households—however, I would venture to guess their kids were not ten years old at the time.

After the damage has been repaired, you start to share these types of stories with others because they are so humorous, after the fact. You find others have their own. One shared by a principal finds Grace coming upon him holding his lunch tray in the hallway. "Would you like to take this tray to the cafeteria for me?" he asks. "No," she replies innocently, not understanding he was really directing her to do it. Luckily, the principal realized the lack of communication between them and was able to laugh at the situation.

In these types of situations, the child could have been viewed as disrespectful without that ever being their intent. This type of thinking also carries over into the character trait terminology that is so often used in disciplining children such as—"be responsible; you need to persevere; show integrity; be courageous." When you are a literal thinker, this terminology is impossible to comprehend unless someone tells you specifically what that entails.

Another area of abstract language that causes these children problems is commands. Early on in schools, it is assumed that very young children understand the directions that are most commonly given. Think about how abstract many of the typical directions are, such as "sit still," "pay attention," and "listen." These are so common and understood by most children, making it hard to believe that children as old as eleven wouldn't understand this. The adults begin to ask themselves, "How could a child who knows so much about so many things not understand a simple direction?" As mothers of these children know, it's hard to explain and have it believed that their child needs specific instruction on what sitting still looks like. In first grade, Joshua repeatedly got in trouble for what the teacher deemed as not paying attention. When I questioned the teacher as to what specific behavior was causing Joshua to lose recess, she said he was not looking at her when she was addressing the class. I later asked Joshua why he did not look at her when she was speaking. He matter-of-factly stated, "Mom, I don't have to look at her to hear what she has to say." Even though he could repeat verbatim what the teacher said, it had to be explained to him what paying attention looked like—i.e. sit, be quiet, look at the person speaking—and that if he acted accordingly the teacher would be able to tell he was hearing her. This still, five years later, continues to be an issue between Joshua and many adults he comes in contact with.

In fifth grade, during a small group presentation about habitats, each child was responsible for reporting to the group about one particular habitat. Joshua would interrupt to tell things he knew about it. He was reminded by the teacher to raise his hand. On the next teacher pass, he was interrupting again. The teacher reminded him a second time to raise his hand. He said, "I did." What he didn't realize was that he needed to wait until she called on him. He just thought his hand in the air gave him permission to talk. When we talked about the situation at home, I explained that this meant he should raise his hand and wait to be called on. Josh replied, "Why didn't she say that?" In his mind, he was complying with her command, but because so much of it was implied and not specific, he didn't understand how to do it correctly.

A further misinterpretation of directions can occur when the child is unable to generalize vocabulary within a direction. Questions on worksheets such as "correct the sentence by rewriting," which really mean "fix the mistakes," are additional sources of confusion. In this particular instance in fifth grade, after looking over his work, I questioned Joshua about his answer. "You didn't make any changes to the sentence." He replied, "I corrected it because I rewrote it." In his mind, he followed the directions and did what was asked of him. The act of rewriting the sentence somehow corrected it.

Examples such as these can be harmless as well as humorous. In second grade, after solving a math problem, a second question asked you to explain why you put the answer that you did. Joshua wrote, "because it's the right one." Not necessarily a wrong answer, but obviously not the explanation the teacher was looking for. Similarly, in fifth grade, when given directions on a science worksheet: "What do you think a botanist does? Use the dictionary," Joshua's response was "a student or expert in botany." "What is botany?" I asked. He confidently replied, "I don't have a clue. I know it's right though, because I used the dictionary like it said." Again, his answer, while not technically wrong, was not the intended one.

As our children get older, the explanations of abstract assignments are not as in-depth because their neurotypical peers don't require it. These children continue to need it and don't often get it, which causes confusion on the purpose of assignments. On the first day of fifth grade, Joshua came home with a homework assignment of a memory basket. It sounded simple enough to put together. The directions sounded pretty straightforward. He was very excited to get started and had very specific ideas on what he wanted to include. First, he needed a memory of something that made him feel warm. Obviously, to him, the answer was a robe. Next, he needed a memory of something that made him laugh. Again, for him, easy—a joke book. Finally, he needed to find something that was "precious as gold." Very confidently, he announces, "The only thing as precious as gold is gold." So, he went up to his room and brought down a gold dollar. Clearly, he was extremely literal in his thinking of what to take. He didn't quite understand the idea of a memory generating a feeling of warmth, laughter, or richness. While the items he chose weren't technically wrong, they didn't capture the intent of the assignment.

Another example of literal interpretation involves the use of compound words as well as homophones and homonyms. All could have multiple meanings, causing a breakdown in comprehension in all areas of language, including reading, writing, and speaking. For example, in history class, the teacher was telling about how pilgrims stuffed their beds with cattails. Grace then enthusiastically made the observation, "I bet you and your husband don't like that idea, since you have cats." After the initial look of confusion, the teacher, realizing Grace thought she meant the real tails of cats, tried to hide her smile and continued on to explain that a cattail is a tall marsh plant with long, brown, fuzzy ends.

Most adults can understand how idioms are a source of confusion. They are often used to give direction such as "bring it down a notch," "knock it off," "let's roll." Idioms are common in everyday communication and the general public assumes they are understood. "Hold your horses." To the vast majority of people, when this expression is used, it means slow down, be patient. My NLD child, in first grade, literally started looking around the room to find the horses she wanted him to hold. This manner of speaking is such an everyday occurrence in modern language. Most of us use these types of idioms countless times during the course of a day. "Hit the road; a dime a dozen; keep your shirt on." When you start to take notice, you realize the frequency with which you use these expressions. No one really has to explain the meaning; we just take their understanding for granted. What if you weren't able to automatically figure out the hidden meaning of these phrases? In order to understand conversations in our society, you must be able to decode what this type of abstract language means.

Misinterpretation works both ways. The inability to communicate can be caused by the misunderstanding on the part of the communication partner, not the child. The child's intent is not understood, so the adult responds in a way the child did not expect. This unexpected response causes the child further confusion in learning how to communicate. The situations can sometimes be more concerning. A perfect example happened one afternoon, while sitting in class. Grace looked up suddenly and asked, "Did the lights just go out?" Given Grace's history of seizures and worried for her safety, the teacher was immediately alarmed, jumped up, and announced, "Let's go! We're out of here!" heading for the school nurse. Pulling her back, Grace said, "No, look. Right there at the end." Sure enough, the end of a long fluorescent bulb had gone dark. However, the rest of the light was working. The teacher's response was based on her understanding of what Grace said, a reverse idiom of sorts.

Other situations that are misunderstood are more innocent and funny. During a speech therapy session, Leslie H-P and Joshua were discussing affection and how it is shown differently depending on the person. For example, some people you would hug lightly, while others, who are closer to you, you would hug tighter. As they were practicing the different types of hugs, Joshua said, "Do you want me to show you how the French kiss?" Without waiting for an answer, Joshua began to move towards Leslie. She had a panic-stricken look on her face, thinking he was going to give her a French kiss, but Joshua kissed her on one cheek and then the other, as they do in some European countries. Puzzled by her reaction, Joshua questioned why she had looked so alarmed. Then came the really interesting part, as one of us was going to have to explain to him the reason for the confusion.

Children diagnosed with neurological disorders often choose to use advanced vocabulary that they sometimes understand but often don't. They use a vocabulary word in the correct situation, in the way it should be used, because they heard it used in another setting. Many times they don't understand what they've said, but the conversation partner assumes they do because it's so confidently presented. Knowledgeable listeners will check for understanding and often find out that their understanding is totally different than what was expected. Again, we ran across this situation during a therapy session. Joshua asked Leslie H-P if she would like to try some passion juice. Everything about how he phrased the question indicated that he totally understood the implication of the word "passion." He said the word with raised eyebrows, leaning in closer to her with a low, soft tone of voice. Leslie replied, quite amused, "Oh, passion juice, sure." At first, we both naturally assumed he was well aware of what "passion" meant, based on his actions. Then, Leslie H-P thought to ask, "What does passion mean, Josh?" "I have no clue," he said, casually setting the cup down and returning to his seat. If Leslie had not asked, all of us would have gone on thinking we were all on the same page. It would have been so easy to miss this lack of communication by not thinking to check for Joshua's grasp of the words he so easily uses.

In this example it's clear that if you don't check for understanding, their misunderstanding is perpetuated and reinforced because they think they did it right. Also, the adults then make an assumption that the child has a knowledge base that they don't really have, and a learning opportunity is missed.

The child's communication partner can generate misunderstandings in selecting the questions they ask. One of the most important things to remember when trying to understand the literal thinking of these children, is to think about the answer you get in relation to the question you asked. Many times this causes such a misunderstanding; it often leads to the child finding himself in an extremely confusing situation that he has no idea how he got in. Unfortunately, they have even less of an ability to rectify the problem because explanations are so very difficult.

On one occasion in fifth grade, I asked Joshua, "What did you miss when you were with the counselor today?" "Nothing," he answered. After thinking about his answer and my question, I decided to restate my inquiry. "What was the rest of the class doing while you were with the counselor?" "Social Studies," he said. He answered the question I asked. In his mind, "I didn't miss anything because I was where I was supposed to be, doing what I was supposed to be doing." He had no idea of the intent behind my question. Thus, I got the information I was looking for, but only after stopping, trying to think like he thinks, and trying again.

Abstract language is everywhere. It's in everything we say, in the text we read, in the movies we watch, in the jokes we tell. It's on posters and sweatshirts and even on street signs. If you're a literal thinker trying to make meaning out of the world that surrounds you, a misunderstanding of abstract language can change the outcome of any event during the course of your day.

Black or white. Yes or no. This is how the child's brain is wired. No gray, no maybe. In the dictionary, literal is defined as "limited to the explicit meaning of a word or text." These very limitations oftentimes lead to one, and only one way, to decode a given situation. Literal thinking can affect not only the child's understanding of the situation, but also the answers they give to questions, as well as their ability to make decisions and problem-solve.

The best way to tackle these issues is to try to think how they think. Know they will answer what you ask. So think about what information you are trying to obtain and ask the question with that in mind. If you're still not sure, rephrase and see if that answer meshes with the first. Most important though, explain, explain, explain. When you or someone else says something, it's safer to *ask* if they understand, than to assume they do. These children become so adept at maintaining the appearance of comprehending so much, that it becomes very hard to tell. Many times you think it's so simple they can't possibly not understand; conversely, when it seems to be higher level, they just might surprise you. My guess, you'll be so surprised by what they *don't* know, what they *do* almost becomes a bonus.

Overall, abstract language understood *literally* greatly diminishes the ability of the child to communicate. When taken in combination with all the other deficits the child is dealing with, the outcome easily becomes rife with numerous problems, ultimately affecting the fragile self-worth of a child who already has many other problems to overcome.

Things to consider

- Think about the questions you asked if you get an unexpected or limited response.

- Don't assume they understand, check for understanding.

- Think about double meanings.

- Consider abstract terms.

- Rephrase questions, directions, commands.

- Explain, explain, explain all abstract language you hear or read.

- Put yourself in their place and try to think in the way they do.

Abstract language—STAT Example 2.1

Step 1: Assess the situation

Running late. Trying to get the kids out the door. Two younger siblings in the van, I say, "Joshua, get in the car." Few seconds later, I turn around, he is still standing there. Using a more emphatic tone, I say again, "Joshua, get in the car!" He just looks at me. "What is the problem?" I yell. "We don't have a car, Mom, we have a van."

Step 2: Develop a hypothesis

Why? Why did they react the way they did? What could they be thinking? Select one or more of the elements below.

• Abstract language	• Motor	• Sensory	• Spatial orientation
• Control/ consistency	• Thinking about others thinking	• Social communication	• Emotions
• Mental flexibility	• Impulsive	• Executive function	• Anxiety

Hypothesis about their thinking (take a guess)

"I can't get into the car because there is no car to get into. What do I do?"
Joshua wants to do what I want him to, but he can't. He doesn't understand that car can mean any vehicle.

Step 3 (optional): Ask questions to obtain a step-by-step account

Types of questions

[Not needed in this example]

 Revise hypothesis. Go back to Step 2

Step 4: Actions to consider

Take action		
Take no action	**Seek additional sources of help**	• educators (teachers, aides, counselors, principal)
Explain	• family members	• support professionals
	• physician (change medication)	• parents of other children
Explain and take action	• neuropsychologist (further assessment)	• friends
		• community resources (social groups)

Explained that I meant whatever vehicle we were taking. So when I said "car," it could also mean "van."

Additional comments

Joshua was paralyzed by the uncertainty of how to proceed. While this seems hard for most people to believe, this type of situation is commonplace for these children with neurological differences. If you aren't thinking like they are, their behavior can appear almost defiant.

Abstract language—STAT Example 2.2

Step 1: Assess the situation

Grace was playing tetherball at recess. An argument arose over whether Grace roped or not. Grace was the only one who felt that she did not break the rule. The teacher intervened asking Grace what she thought the rule was. She said, "If you touch the rope, you're out. I didn't touch the rope, I touched the chain connecting the rope to the ball."

Step 2: Develop a hypothesis

Why? Why did they react the way they did? What could they be thinking? Select one or more of the elements below.

• Abstract language	• Motor	• Sensory	• Spatial orientation
• Control/ consistency	• Thinking about others thinking	• Social communication	• Emotions
• Mental flexibility	• Impulsive	• Executive function	• Anxiety

Hypothesis about their thinking (take a guess)

The teacher realized Grace had a very literal understanding of the situation. In his mind, *"The rule is if you touch the rope you are out. I did not touch the rope. I touched the chain. Therefore, I am not out."*

Step 3 (optional): Ask questions to obtain a step-by-step account

Types of questions

[Not needed in this example]

 Revise hypothesis. Go back to Step 2

Step 4: Actions to consider		
Take action	**Seek additional sources of help**	• educators (teachers, aides, counselors, principal)
Take no action	• family members • physician (change medication) • neuropsychologist (further assessment)	• support professionals • parents of other children • friends • community resources (social groups)
Explain		
Explain and take action		

The teacher explained to Grace that really the rule was if you touch anything other than the ball you're out, therefore, she did break the rule and was out. She also was able to take action by smoothing over the situation with her peers explaining to them that Grace just didn't understand what the rule really was.

Additional comments

Possibly this could have the the teacher's "aha" moment. Because of previous discussions about Grace, she was able to accurately assess the situation, not automatically assuming it to be a behavior problem on Grace's part. The teacher now knew to ask follow-up questions and look for how Grace's literal under-standing was affecting the situation. An immediate effect was made on Grace's life by averting a potentially bad situation. Because of the teacher's position, many other children's lives have the chance to also be positively impacted. In the future, as she continues to apply this new way of thinking with other children, teachers, and staff, the potential exists for this one encounter to have an exponential effect, the benefits of which could be felt for many years to come.

Abstract language—STAT Example 2.3

Step 1: Assess the situation
Joshua called home in tears. Says he's done something horrible. Took something that did not belong to him. A pencil.

Step 2: Develop a hypothesis

Why? Why did they react the way they did? What could they be thinking? Select one or more of the elements below.

• Abstract language	• Motor	• Sensory	• Spatial orientation
• Control/ consistency	• Thinking about others thinking	• Social communication	• Emotions
• Mental flexibility	• Impulsive	• Executive function	• Anxiety

Hypothesis about their thinking (take a guess)

"That's a cool pencil, I'd like to have it." Saw something he really wanted and took it.

Step 3 (optional): Ask questions to obtain a step-by-step account

Types of questions

"Tell me exactly what happened. You were sitting at your desk, then what happened?" Joshua says, "**I got up to sharpen my pencil.**" "And you picked up a pencil off somebody's desk?" "**No, I found it on the floor. Then I went back and sat down,**" he said. "Then what?" "**Andrew told the teacher I stole his pencil.**" "Then what?" "**Then the teacher came up and said, 'Josh, is that your pencil?'**" "What did you say?" "**I said, 'No'.**"

 Revise hypothesis. Go back to Step 2

Step 2: Develop a hypothesis

Why? Why did they react the way they did? What could they be thinking? Select one or more of the elements below.

• Abstract language	• Motor	• Sensory	• Spatial orientation
• Control/ consistency	• Thinking about others thinking	• Social communication	• Emotions
• Mental flexibility	• ~~Impulsive~~	• Executive function	• Anxiety

Hypothesis about their thinking (take a guess)

"I answered the question she asked. Why am I getting blamed for something I didn't do." Took teacher's question literally. Didn't understand she was asking him if he stole the pencil. Likewise, the teacher did not realize there had been a breakdown in communication and that she did not have the information she was looking for.

Step 4: Actions to consider

Take action	**Seek additional sources of help**	• educators (teachers, aides, counselors, principal)
Take no action	• family members	• support professionals
Explain	• physician (change medication)	• parents of other children
Explain and take action	• neuropsychologist (further assessment)	• friends
		• community resources (social groups)

Explained to Josh the teacher's thinking. She really meant, "Did you take something that didn't belong to you? Did you steal that pencil?"

Took action with the teacher. Explained Joshua's thinking to the teacher. He answered her question literally, not understanding. Next time, ask the question you want answered. Did you steal the pencil? My goal was to make sure she understood that Joshua was not being deceitful, nor was he a thief.

Additional comments

With that two-sentence exchange, the entire situation became clear. All because Joshua answered what I asked and I just happened to ask the right questions. I'm sure Joshua was quite befuddled as to what he did that was so "horrible" that day. Nobody ever told him picking something up off the floor was grounds for a phone call home. No wonder the child feels like he's "always getting blamed for things he doesn't do." His inability to correctly problem-solve the situation is one problem, his inability to explain the misunderstanding is another. Both were compounded by the question that was asked. He answered what was asked.

There are numerous examples of disruptive "answer what you ask" scenarios in the lives of these children. Unfortunately, they have the potential to cause great damage to the child's self-esteem, not to mention their anxiety level.

Chapter 3

Motor

"Sometimes the kids make fun of me when I can't do things as good as they can"—Joshua, at the prospect of having to participate in gym on a daily basis.

Who would have thought that one child's motor deficits could impact the decisions made for an entire family? When my three boys were taking swimming lessons, Danny, Joshua's younger brother, progressed through the swimming levels at a faster rate than Joshua did, eventually catching up with him. At the time of the next registration, Joshua refused to continue with the lessons because Danny would have been promoted to the next level above him. As a result, I chose to discontinue the lessons at that time because it was causing a strain on the boys' relationship. At first glance the motor skills area seems to be an isolated one, dealt with individually, with few far-reaching affects. However, Joshua's motor skills caused a change not only in his life, but also impacted the lives of the other two boys.

Many people who have children are familiar with motor development from reading child development books, visiting the doctor, and discussions with teachers at school. Problems in the motor area are more easily identified because they are more obvious to the observer. When children have neurological differences, motor difficulties seem to be the earliest, most identifiable problems exhibited. This transparency allows parents to receive services more readily because the presence of a deficit is not questioned. The motor area tends to be a bit more black-and-white, requiring less explanation and proof on the parents' part.

The motor area is intricately related to the areas of spatial orientation and sensory. As children move through their world, they use these three areas simultaneously. Even though this is the case, we have decided to address each area separately on the STAT. These three areas can stand alone or act as one, consequently playing a part in the same problem. However, when systematically thinking through the problem, it is easier to problem-solve and develop accommodations by thinking about the individual contribution of each area.

As we discuss this topic, we will divide the section into the typical categories of fine and gross motor skills. As with all the areas on the STAT, the degree to which each child is affected is on a continuum. Motor skills are no exception. Whereas one child may never master one area, it may never present itself as an issue for another child with the same diagnosis. For example, Joshua was late in acquiring the skill of bike riding, but did eventually develop that skill, even to the extent of being able to jump ramps. In Grace's case, however, she was never able to develop this skill and probably never will. It's really a matter of degrees.

Oftentimes children with neurological differences are easily discernible by the manner in which they walk or run. In Joshua's case, his steps are heavy, his body moves in a stiff manner as if it is one part, instead of separate parts moving in synchrony. For Grace, walking is a safety issue because she must constantly struggle to maintain her balance. Each has a motor skill deficit in walking that impacts them differently, one being cosmetic, the other a matter of safety. Both, however, can be identified when compared to their typical peers.

Because Grace's issues are more safety-related and her difficulty is with maintaining her balance, every environment has the potential to become a virtual minefield. Cracks in the sidewalk causing an uneven surface, any kind of slope in the terrain, a curb, steps, or a crowded hallway, all are obstacles that need to be addressed. When one considers daily functioning, the motor issues to be managed for Grace are mainly physical, while Joshua's management issues focus more on the emotional effects.

So many of the activities that offer children an opportunity to develop friendships revolve around activities that require physical prowess. From pre-school through high school, much of a child's world is set up for physical activity. Extra-curricular activities are focused on team sports such as basketball, baseball, soccer, and football. In school, gym class and recess are designed for physical activity. Parents focus on developing their children's motor skills early with tricycles and swingsets in an effort to promote that development. While this is an important and necessary point of emphasis, it puts the neurologically different child with motor challenges at a significant disadvantage socially. When a child's gross motor skills are so significantly impaired, it limits the amount and type of social interaction they are able to have with their neurotypical peers, which can ultimately have a negative effect on their social emotional well-being.

In Joshua's situation, because his disability isn't as obvious, he becomes a likely target for ridicule by his classmates. At the prospect of having to participate in gym on a daily basis in his sixth grade year, Joshua's increasing level of anxiety was evident. In the process of talking him through it, I asked him if he thought he needed an aide with him in that class. He responded that he did. I proceeded to ask him why he felt he needed one, and he said he needed one "in case something went wrong." I asked him what might go wrong. He said, "Sometimes the kids make fun of me when I can't do things as good as they can." I asked, "Do they say stuff to you?" "They mostly laugh at me and whisper comments to each other." So many children look forward to gym and recess during the course of a school day. However, those times for neurologically different children can be a cause of great anxiety, a virtual nightmare.

Sometimes a parent sees an activity and knows immediately that their child is not able to participate. It's important, however, to look at each situation individually with a careful eye. Parents shouldn't rush to judgement, if there is a chance their child could happily participate. Take, for instance, a child who is not adept at basketball. It would be incorrect to assume he could not excel at soccer. Both require gross motor skills, but because those skills are used for different purposes, in different ways, making an incorrect assumption could deny a child his chance to enjoy a social event.

As parents consider motor activities for their children, they may want to determine the extent to which their child is able to participate and what they hope to gain from the experience. For example, Joshua showed an interest in participating in basketball. I wanted to encourage that interest while providing a positive experience. Therefore, it was important to find a league that placed more of an emphasis on recreation. My goals for him were to increase his opportunity for social interaction, while getting some exercise, and enjoying the sense of being part of a team. Because he continued to enjoy going and was able to participate at an equivalent level to the other kids, I felt sure it was a good choice. It really comes down to finding a good match.

The flip side of gross motor is fine motor. An emphasis on fine motor deficits begins to rear its ugly head when children enter pre-school. At this stage there is a focus on self-help skills such as zipping and buttoning, as well as artistic skills such as coloring and cutting. Many people can relate to feelings parents have as they inspect the pictures displayed in the hall, trying to find their child's master-piece, only to realize it is the worst one of the entire class. There you are, huddled with your family around this picture, ooing and aahing about its merits, while your stomach churns as you realize how far from the norm your child's fine motor skills really are. At the pre-school level, the inability to do these tasks is met with minimal resistance and a request to continue trying. However, as early as kindergarten, expectations increase and teachers begin to confer with parents about the need for their child to color in the lines and cut with more precision. As your child continues through school, handwriting becomes the next hurdle. At parent conferences, your child's fine motor deficits are repeatedly brought to your attention, with minimal suggestions on ways to help. Consequently, your child is continually penalized academically, not to mention the emotional impact that repeated comments such as "neater," "messy," and "watch your handwriting" have on a child's self-esteem. Teachers appear to have a difficulty in believing this is not a choice and beyond the child's control. It's like asking someone with a broken arm to bend it. They would if they could, but they can't. How frustrating and degrading it must feel to continue to try unsuccessfully to complete a task to someone else's satisfaction.

At each age level parents need to determine where fine motor issues may arise and do their best to determine the accommodations that can be made to reduce their child's anxiety, as well as the impact on their self-esteem. Tying shoes continues to be an issue for many children. They often learn to tie their shoes eventually—but not tightly enough. While asking for help at kindergar-ten is somewhat tolerated, later it will certainly be met with disbelief or a judge-ment that the child is lazy.

Eating skills continue to be an issue much longer than would be the case with a typically developing child. Manipulating utensils to cut food can some-times present a problem, as it makes it more evident that there is an underlying issue. When you're the only parent at a table cutting your child's food, others have a tendency to assume either that you are babying your child, and/or that your child is lazy. At mealtimes they are the one with food stains around their mouth and on their clothes. On an outing at an amusement park with Grace, her mother looked across and saw her sitting on a bench with a big, beautiful, red snow cone. As she looked more closely, it was no surprise that the stain of the snow cone had made its way onto Grace's clean white shirt, and that her lovely red lips appeared swollen, surrounded by all that red. Moments like these remind you that you need to laugh, share your child's joy, and forget about what other people think.

Once into middle school, maneuvering the combination lock on a locker can be an area of concern. The physical act of opening the lock is difficult in and of itself—however, aggravated by time constraints, anxiety levels can quickly rise. Schools seem willing to provide accommodations in this area, but they need to be informed. Handwriting, on the other hand, continues to be an issue throughout school, causing some students' grades to plummet even though they have a grasp of the material. Poor handwriting can cause points to be lost easily, depending on the teacher. Additionally, so many school projects include an art component with points attached. For instance, in third grade Joshua had an assignment, in reading, of creating a travel brochure. He received a C, which didn't surprise me at the time because I knew his drawing and coloring skills were not in the gifted range. However, when he received a lower reading grade than I expected, I immediately emailed the teacher to find out why. She informed me that "Yes, his reading is excellent" but that he didn't do well on two assignments that were weighted more heavily, one being the travel brochure. At that point, I remember asking myself, "How can he receive a low grade in reading because he can't draw or color?" To this day, I haven't gotten an answer to that question. It is always so frustrating when your child works diligently to complete an assignment that is difficult for him, as well as unpleasant, only to have his self-esteem and grade deflated.

Although fine motor skills may be a problem with some tasks, this doesn't necessarily mean they are affected across the board. Depending on the child, an individual can often be adept at playing video games, typing, or even playing the piano. That's why it's important to look at each child individually and allow them to try new things that have the potential for success.

When thinking about motor deficits, one might wonder which of gross or fine motor skills has a bigger impact on the emotional psyche of the child and the family. There may be cause for debate about this, but there is no debate that each is a significant area to be considered when trying to improve the quality of your child's life. It often seems that gross motor concerns cause more difficulty when it comes to forging relationships with peers, while fine motor concerns seem to cause more difficulty in the school arena. There really is no question that both fine and gross motor deficits spill over into the emotional well-being of the child and family.

Things to consider

- Analyze the environment for possible safety concerns.
- Survey the environment with the child, pointing out potentially dangerous areas.
- When selecting activities involving motor skills, decide what benefits engaging in this activity will have for your child (social, emotional, physical).
- Let them participate in activities to the extent they are able, exposing them to different activities, and discussing their interest.
- Don't rule out sports altogether if team sports don't work. Consider individual sports such as golf, archery, horseback riding, etc., as well as other social outlets such as chess club, band, newspaper, etc.

Motor—STAT Example 3.1

Step 1: Assess the situation

Joshua's teacher sent a note home stating that he was lying on the floor by his desk to do his work. The teacher indicated that if she asked him to sit in his seat, he would for a short time, but would eventually return to completing his work on the floor.

Step 2: Develop a hypothesis

Why? Why did they react the way they did? What could they be thinking? Select one or more of the elements below.

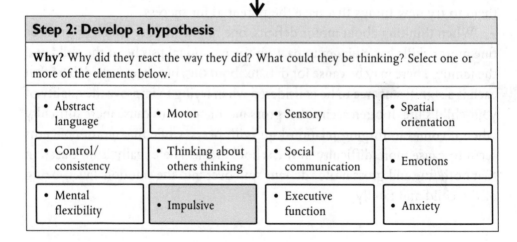

• Abstract language	• Motor	• Sensory	• Spatial orientation
• Control/ consistency	• Thinking about others thinking	• Social communication	• Emotions
• Mental flexibility	• Impulsive	• Executive function	• Anxiety

Hypothesis about their thinking (take a guess)

"I don't feel like sitting at my desk. I think I'll just lie on the floor." Didn't think about how it would look or impact on the teachers or others in the class.

Step 3 (optional): Ask questions to obtain a step-by-step account

Types of questions

"Why were you on the floor?" **"Because it's easier for me to write that way."** "Did you tell her that?" **"Yes, but she didn't care."**

 Revise hypothesis. Go back to Step 2

Step 2: Develop a hypothesis

Why? Why did they react the way they did? What could they be thinking? Select one or more of the elements below.

• Abstract language	• Motor	• Sensory	• Spatial orientation
• Control/ consistency	• Thinking about others thinking	• Social communication	• Emotions
• Mental flexibility	• ~~Impulsive~~	• Executive function	• Anxiety

Hypothesis about their thinking (take a guess)

"When I lie on the floor, it's easier for me to write." Having the body stable makes fine motor tasks easier.

Step 4: Actions to consider

Take action

Take no action

Explain

Explain and take action

Seek additional sources of help

- family members
- physician (change medication)
- neuropsychologist (further assessment)

- educators (teachers, aides, counselors, principal)
- support professionals
- parents of other children
- friends
- community resources (social groups)

Explain Joshua's thinking to the teacher. Discuss with the teacher that Joshua's action is the result of a body in space issue, not a behavioral one. Stabilizing his body makes handwriting easier. Work to develop appropriate accommodations and consider consulting an occupational therapist.

Additional comments

Initially when the teacher sent the note home, I quickly thought about why Joshua would want to lie on the floor to write. I really didn't spend much time analyzing the situation, and simply asked Josh why he was choosing to do this. His response, indicating that it was easier for him, led me to consider the 12 possibilities in Step 2 of STAT. In reviewing these choices, I was able to narrow it down to a combination of causes, which included motor and spatial orientation. Because of previous conversations with occupational therapists, I knew that lying on the floor made the act of writing easier, since Josh was able to stabilize his body, knowing where it was in space. In this circumstance, the teacher may have viewed this behavior as attention-seeking or defiant, when in reality it was a necessity. Once again, this demonstrates that the behavior exhibited is not without reason or purpose.

Chapter 4

Sensory

"Mom, there is an ear-shattering noise in the basement!" Joshua frantically yells, upon hearing what turns out to be a cricket.

Think for a moment about a bar of Irish Spring soap. How many kids do you know that would request it as a gift and be overjoyed upon receiving it? Joshua was thrilled to receive his Christmas gift from Leslie H-P, which consisted of money, a dark chocolate candy bar, a can of olives, and a bar of Irish Spring soap. It was obvious the soap was the biggest hit, as he immediately tore into it. Obviously this assortment of gifts is not on the typical ten-year-old's list. This highlights the importance that sensory issues have in enhancing the quality of life for a child with neurological differences. One wouldn't think sensory issues would play such an important part in a child's life, but there is no question that they do.

Your senses impact the quality of your life and your ability to enjoy it. Your senses are essential in making you feel alive. Senses dictate how you obtain feedback from your environment and how you perceive the world. When you encounter a person who has lost their sense of sight or hearing, you can recognize the impact and empathize with how that person is forced to function in the world. While children diagnosed with neurological differences may be fortunate enough not to have had an entire sensory system wiped out, they may often have more than one of their sensory systems affected to varying degrees. This impacts their ability to function in the world, but goes largely unrecognized as having a significant impact on their lives.

The sensory systems of these children are often wired differently than those of their typical peers. Oftentimes their sensory systems are programmed to receive input at the extreme ends of a continuum. They can have a hyper- or hypo-response to input received through their system. Each child's response to various stimuli is different and very individualized. So, no single sweeping statement can be made as to how children will respond. It is important for parents and educators to consider the way that sensory input is received in an effort to effectively assess troublesome situations. Once again, the actions of the child can be misinterpreted if the sensory issues are not considered. Their behavior can be seen as socially inappropriate, manipulative, and even defiant, causing punitive consequences. Punishment in these circumstances is totally ineffective because it doesn't address the root of the problem. The child doesn't know that the way they perceive the world is different from that of those around them. This problem can be pervasive and affect many areas of their life, like hygiene, nutrition, how they show affection, their tolerance for pain, their ability to function in a given environment, and how others perceive them socially. How they receive sensory input affects their perception of the situation and, therefore, the decisions they make as a result.

At some point, every parent has had clothing battles with their child over an irritating tag on the back of a shirt, an uncomfortable sock seam, or a scratchy sweater. These are sensory issues that also impact neurotypical children to a certain degree. However, for a neurotypical child most often the fix is a simple one. On the other hand, with children with neurological differences, these circumstances could easily lead to a meltdown that makes moving forward impossible. Joshua continually seems to have sock issues. We went through a phase when no sock seemed to be satisfactory, for one reason or another. Finally, after many attempts and much expense, we stumbled upon what evidently was the perfect sock. This is a great feeling, until you realize the pressure that you are immediately put under to make sure they are always clean and readily available. Don't even think you're going to be able to get by with "Can't you wear these just this once until I have a chance to wash the other ones?" It won't work. When you find something that works, buy in bulk.

Parents of kids with neurological problems are well aware that simple tasks of daily hygiene, such as brushing their teeth or taking a shower, can consume enormous chunks of your day. It's not as simple as requesting your child to go brush their teeth or wash their hair. You, as the parent, may need to plan large chunks of time, coaxing your child into and through the process, as well as supervising and actively engaging in it. For the parents, it can be exhausting and frustrating when one considers it is only a small part of a day that will surely be filled with continual hurdles. From the child's perspective, the mere mention of the task causes anxiety to build in anticipation of the physical pain associated with those tasks. The beads of water, to them, can feel like hailstones, while the bristles of a toothbrush can feel as if they are piercing their gums.

While they can feel extremes of pain when engaging in simple tasks, often they don't feel pain in circumstances where neurotypical children would. Joshua, on more than one occasion, would come in from playing outside with a stream of dried blood down his leg. Everything was fine until I asked him what had happened, at which he would look from his knee to me with an expression of horror on his face, screaming, "Oh my gosh! My knee! It hurts so bad!" For the next few hours, he would be nearly inconsolable due to the level of pain he obviously thought he was in—once he realized he was hurt. Another telling example occurred on occasion at Grace's school. Attempting to walk through a doorway, she would misjudge where her body was in space and slam into the frame of the door with her shoulder—hard, very hard. Any other child, or adult for that matter, would not have been able to hide what was certainly immense pain. Seeing the sheer force of the blow would cause anyone to wince in empathetic pain. Oddly enough, Grace never even broke stride or changed pace in the least. She literally bounced off the frame, continuing as if nothing had gotten in her way, and certainly was not slowed down at all. When asked if she was all right, she would look almost perplexed, as if to say, "Why wouldn't I be?" She didn't appear to even have noticed.

Sensory issues affect not only what the child eats, but also how they eat. Eating for them is not simply about taste; it also is about texture and smell. Sometimes they have a craving for particular taste and take it to an extreme. For instance, Joshua likes to request a bowl of lemon slices at a restaurant and ceremoniously savors it while repeatedly making lemons the topic of conversation. Preferences are often specific, including brands, as well as how the food is served. If the favourite item is not readily available, the potential for upset exists. For Christmas one year, Grace's most prized gift was a long pickle fork. It was to be used only by her, so that she could access every last pickle from her huge, personal jars. Of course, what typical child wouldn't be equally ecstatic to receive their very own pickle fork? Sensory[AQ] also affects the way children eat, and can have an impact on other's perception of their manners. It is always fascinating at dinner to watch Joshua and Grace wipe their forks off in between bites, or lift their string of spaghetti high above their head to systematically suck it in like a bird eating a worm—of course, with accompanying sound effects.

Also, the scents that surround us are a big part of our world—as is evidenced by the perfume industry. For children with neurological differences, everyday scents have as much importance as an expensive perfume may for others. What may appear to be an unimportant item can become a coveted gift. On vacation one year, our family went to a dinner show. With our utensils came prepackaged handwipes to be used when you finished your meal. The sixty dollars apiece we paid to be there didn't have nearly the impact on Joshua that these wipes did. For him it was, literally, the hit of the evening and quite possibly the trip. We continued to hear about how fantastic these wipes smelled, how the lemon scent made him feel so relaxed, and didn't we enjoy them as much as him—over and over and over again. I, however, did not appreciate the significance of the wipes until we began our twelve-hour drive home. I'm sure in any family that is traveling by car for an extended period of time, the trip can be trying for the parents. In our family, with three boys, one being Joshua, it makes for an extremely volatile atmosphere, with the possibility of confrontation becoming a very real likelihood. However, stocked with all the unopened wipes he had picked up off the tables as we left that night, our trip was, quite surprisingly, rather uneventful. One by one, Joshua would open a package and carefully place the blessed lemon-scented wipe over his face. The impact that wipe had on the happiness of our entire family for the drive home cannot be done justice when described only in words. That scent of lemon achieved a level of serenity that can only be repeated—if you have an unlimited supply. Consequently, after weeks of unrelenting persistence on Joshua's part, I made the executive decision that for my own sanity, we needed to figure out how to reproduce this scent. After buying numerous air fresheners in many different forms, it was quite obvious nothing was going to equal the original. Luckily for me, I had thought to save one wipe in case of emergency. Even luckier for me, the manufacturer's website was on it. As if searching for the unobtainable gift of the season, I proceeded to track down these exact wipes with a fervor and intensity that could not be matched. Eventually, after literally weeks of correspondence with the manufacturer, and hundreds of questions from Joshua as to the status of the order, the package finally arrived. After surviving the initial disappointment that the wording on the outside of each individual package was different from that on the ones we had had on vacation, I was finally able to convince Joshua that the scents were, in fact, exactly the same. While this story focuses on just one of the senses, it accurately illustrates the importance, to the child, that any sensory issue can play in their lives, as well as the extent to which parents may need to be willing to go in dealing with them.

Most people are able to block out insignificant background noise, but this is often not the case for children with neurological differences, because what they hear and how they hear it is different. As Leslie H-P sat working with Joshua during a session, it was clear he had become totally distracted, looking around the room. When she asked him what was wrong, Joshua said, "Don't you hear that?" "Hear what?" "That fly!" Once we began to listen, we too heard it. He heard the buzz of that fly so loudly and was so distracted by the sound, that it made it nearly impossible for him to concentrate. From a very young age, Joshua also seemed to have the ability to hear sounds from very far away. Many times, we would be outside and he would say, "Mommy, here comes the icecream man," or "Do you hear the ambulance?" or "Where is the jet?" Every time, I would say, "What? The icecream man isn't here," or "What siren?" or "I don't see a jet." Inevitably, minutes later, here came the icecream man, the fire truck, or a jet would fly overhead. Each and every time, I was amazed at the amount of time that elapsed between when he heard it and when I did.

This hypersensitivity to sound unfortunately started to impact the social situations in which Joshua was willing to participate. Joshua's friend, Nick, had an annual end-of-summer campout where six or seven boys were invited and they would pitch tents in the backyard. Every year Joshua went without incident. However, when he was ten something changed his awareness of the sounds that he was hearing outside as he was trying to get to sleep. The sounds made it unbearable for him. The more he focused on the sounds, the louder they got, and the more his anxiety increased, making it impossible for him to relax enough to get to sleep. After he had taken as much as he could bear, Jane, Nick's mom, suggested he sleep in Nick's room for the night. This was a wonderful solution that enabled him to stay and to participate in the morning, but the intensity of the noise with the resulting increase in anxiety stuck with Joshua so that the next summer he decided not to go. When I asked him why, he said, "Because the sounds that the crickets make are so loud and I can't get to sleep, and then I get upset." It was sad for him to sacrifice a social event that he otherwise thoroughly enjoyed, because of a sensory issue. Ultimately, we came up with the solution of going for the evening and picking him up when everyone else was getting ready for bed. Because Nick knew from the start, it wasn't a disappointment to him, and Joshua was able to go and enjoy the evening without the possibility of an anxiety-filled situation lying ahead. This story shows how drastically sensory issues can impact the course of a child's life and the choices they consequently make.

Sensory issues can cause the child to be perceived negatively by others. This comes into play with everyday simple actions that they take. Something as simple as closing a door can be misconstrued, because what they actually do is slam it, so that if you don't understand that they can't feel how hard they are closing it, you may perceive them as being angry, upset, destructive, or defiant. Their attempts at showing affection can often be painful for the recipient: since a pat on the back turns into a slap and a hug can feel like the crush of a boa constrictor, the reaction they receive doesn't always match their original attempt, and what was meant to be a friendly pat on the back to a peer, could result in a trip to the principal's office.

If parents are not aware of the significance of sensory issues, they may tend to misinterpret and downplay their impact. For instance, one evening Michael, Joshua's brother, was slurping his soup as he ate. Although no one else seemed to notice, Joshua was extremely irritated, repeatedly yelling at Michael to stop. It would have been easy for me to dismiss it. It truly was not that loud, so I was inclined to tell Joshua to ignore it. In my mind I'm thinking, "It's not that irritating to me, so how could it be that bad for him." However, if I heard the sound as he did, I would certainly have been just as disturbed. By looking at the situation through his eyes, or in this case, hearing it through his ears, and magnifying the sound one hundredfold, I could begin to empathize with his level of frustration. So instead of telling Joshua to get over it, I told Michael to stop. In the end, it was good for Michael's manners, as well as Joshua's sanity.

While it varies from child to child, hypersensitive hearing is the sensory area that has definitely led to many areas of difficulty in our house. For instance, last summer, Joshua decided the fan in his room had apparently begun to make a sound. At first hearing, I wasn't able to decipher any sound out of the ordinary. After his repeated insistence that there was in fact a noise being made, I listened very carefully and was able to make out what, to me, was a slight tapping sound as the fan rotated. Again, my first instinct was to tell him to ignore it and go to sleep. However, to him, the sound was so loud and disturbing that there was no way to ignore it and go to sleep. With each passing turn of the fan, Joshua's anxiety intensified, finally culminating in tears because he wasn't able to sleep. As Todd, Joshua's father, was out of town, my dad graciously agreed to come and take a look. After three separate attempts, one of which required taking the fan completely out of the ceiling, it passed inspection. Although it was extremely inconvenient, required much patience, and was very time-consuming, it was worth it when finally Joshua could relax and fall asleep normally. The length to which you are willing to go to rectify these situations exemplifies the negative impact they can have on your child's life. Sometimes it requires the parent to believe what the child reports and a willingness to try to resolve the circumstances around the sensory upset, when it really seems insignificant. For the child, the problem is real.

There are times when all the sensory systems are impacted at once, causing overload. Different children express sensory overload in different ways. Some children look as if they are staring, but in reality, it is their way of compensating. It seems that when too many systems are stimulated at once and they can't absorb and process all that is going on around them, their system has no choice but to somehow shut down. This became apparent with Grace every time she went to a movie or play. Wanting to plan a special family event, her family bought tickets to the play *The Lion King*. As they were waiting for the curtain to rise, their anticipation built for what they were sure was going to be a wonderful time spent together, being able to watch Grace enjoy her first experience at a play. The curtain rose on what is a fabulous opening with all the exotic characters dancing to the buildup of the music. Upon looking over, totally expecting to see Grace with an awestruck look of pleasure on her face, the family found instead that she was asleep. A mix of emotions fell over the family, as they were frustrated, sad, and disappointed that she didn't feel the joy they had hoped she would feel. While their expectations of the night, of being able to share that experience with her, were not met by what actually happened, Grace was nonetheless happy to have been part of the event. When asked what she thought about the play, she enthusiastically replied, "Oh, it was great!" In reality, all that was going on was just too much input for her sensory system and it was forced to shut down.

A similar situation happened with Joshua. Being University of Kentucky basketball fans is a standing tradition in my family. As part of coming of age, you are blessed with the opportunity to travel to Lexington to witness, in person, your first University of Kentucky basketball game. It is quite a momentous event, surrounded with great anticipation. As Joshua was turning eleven this year, we thought that because of his consistent support over the years he had finally earned the right to make the trip. We got the tickets, planned the day, and looked forward to it with much eagerness. On game day, you could feel the excitement build throughout the day, especially as we got closer and closer. As we were walking into Rupp Arena, Joshua began mumbling to himself. This should have been my first clue that things might not go like I had planned. As we entered the seating area, Joshua immediately took three steps back, obviously stunned by the presence of the 23,000 people he was sharing a room with. Walking up the stadium steps was difficult for him, as they were smaller and closer together than regular stairs. As we got to our seats located very near the top, Joshua looked down and said, "I didn't know I was afraid of heights." For those of you who have attended similar events, you know it is a different feeling, almost disconcerting, to be so high, looking down on something so small that looks so big on television. As the game was about to begin, Joshua commented, "I think I feel very uncomfortable around all these people." With all the fans on their feet, screaming, the noise level increased as the game started. He then said in my ear in a panicked voice, "My ears just can't take anymore." As the first basket was scored, I turned to give him the obligatory high five. Instead of being met by an overjoyed little boy taking in everything happening around him, what I found was an overwhelmed little boy sitting down, with the hood of his sweatshirt pulled tightly over his head, and his body in a cocoon-type position. Something that was so important to me, something I had long looked forward to sharing with my son, had me leaving the arena thinking dejectedly, "Why does this (NLD) have to affect everything?"

Figuring out what your child needs in terms of sensory is not a one-time thing. Just when you think you've determined what your child's sensory needs and surrounding issues are, their systems develop and change and you find that some things get better while others get worse. Parents are faced with the continuing challenge of determining and dealing with their child's sensory needs on an ongoing basis. The child's sensory wiring requires families and educators to see and think about the environment the child is in from the child's point of view. It is necessary to believe that each child has reasons to act in the manner they do. It's the job of those who love them to determine the why of their behavior and consider sensory is as one of the possibilities.

Things to consider

- It's important to pick your battles. Ask yourself, "How important is this?"
- If it doesn't impact someone else negatively, let it go (e.g. clothing choices, soap choices).
- Think about how an environmental change will help the child to cope (e.g. does it help them sleep better, reduce anxiety).
- Put yourself in their environment and think about how you would react if your senses were hypo or hyper.
- Explain to the child how they're sensing the world differently than others.

Sensory—STAT Example 4.1

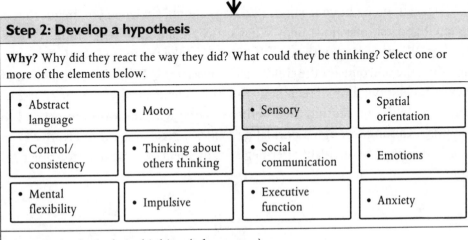

Step 1: Assess the situation
It's summertime. I go in to tuck Joshua in. His windows are closed. His room is sweltering. I say "Why are your windows closed?" as I proceed to open them. He says, "It's too loud out there. I won't be able to get to sleep." I'm listening outside but don't hear anything that would be disturbing to me. Because of our experience with the campout previously discussed in this chapter, I realized that what he heard were the crickets.

Step 2: Develop a hypothesis
Why? Why did they react the way they did? What could they be thinking? Select one or more of the elements below.

• Abstract language	• Motor	• Sensory	• Spatial orientation
• Control/ consistency	• Thinking about others thinking	• Social communication	• Emotions
• Mental flexibility	• Impulsive	• Executive function	• Anxiety

Hypothesis about their thinking (take a guess)

"I need to get to sleep. I won't be able to do this with the loud sounds these crickets are making."—resulting in an increase in anxiety.

Step 3 (optional): Ask questions to obtain a step-by-step account

Types of questions

"What is it that you hear? I don't hear anything."

"Could it be the crickets again?"

"Can you ignore it?"

Revise hypothesis. Go back to Step 2

Step 4: Actions to consider

Take action	**Seek additional sources of help**	• educators (teachers, aides, counselors, principal)
Take no action	• family members	• support professionals
	• physician (change medication)	• parents of other children
Explain		• friends
	• neuropsychologist (further assessment)	• community resources (social groups)
Explain and take action		

Closed windows and turned up the fan.

Additional comments

If you encounter this situation with a typical child who has no sensory issues, the usual reaction from a parent would be to go into the room, open the windows, and tell the child to ignore the noise and go to sleep. Parents of children with neurological differences will have moments like this one when red flags will go up in your mind. Red flags should fly when you begin to feel agitated and ask questions like "What's this all about?" "Why would you do that" or "What's wrong with you?" If you don't take the time to think about the situation, the outcome for the child can be devastating. From the child's point of view, the compounding of seemingly minor incidents throughout the course of a day can build up, causing their ability to cope with the world in general to diminish. Getting through a normal day takes a great amount of effort. When faced with negative incident after negative incident, the capacity to cope runs dry.

Sensory—STAT Example 4.2

Step 1: Assess the situation

Grace walks into her aunt's house and greets her uncle with a "pat" on the back, along with a verbal greeting, "Hi, Ted." Ted's face grimaces with the simultaneous arching of his back.

Step 2: Develop a hypothesis

Why? Why did they react the way they did? What could they be thinking? Select one or more of the elements below.

• Abstract language	• Motor	• Sensory	• Spatial orientation
• Control/ consistency	• Thinking about others thinking	• Social communication	• Emotions
• Mental flexibility	• Impulsive	• Executive function	• Anxiety

Hypothesis about their thinking (take a guess)

"There's Ted. I'm happy to see him, so I'm going to give him big hello." It's obvious she wants to greet you in a friendly way, but you don't understand why she hit you so hard.

Step 3 (optional): Ask questions to obtain a step-by-step account

Types of questions

"Why did you hit me so hard?" "Did you mean to hurt me?"

 Revise hypothesis. Go back to Step 2

Step 4: Actions to consider

Take action

Take no action

Explain

Explain and take action

Seek additional sources of help

- family members
- physician (change medication)
- neuropsychologist (further assessment)

- educators (teachers, aides, counselors, principal)
- support professionals
- parents of other children
- friends
- community resources (social groups)

"You hit harder than you realize you are hitting. When you think you're patting someone, to them it feels like a hit. It hurts them. I know you don't want to hurt people, so let's practice how you can pat them." Physically touching them can help them to better understand and feel the difference.

Additional comments

In an attempt to greet someone in a friendly fashion, Grace "pats" someone on the back and says hello. However, she is unaware that her pat is delivered with extreme force. Her intent of having a friendly exchange is unintentionally sabotaged.

After being patted on the back with extreme force a number of times, and responding quite loudly with "Oh, that hurts!" you realize, because they continue to act in the same manner, that they don't understand what needs to change. When you say that it hurts, you are assuming they understand the implied message, but they don't. It's then you begin to ask them, "Why did you hit me so hard? Did you mean to hurt me?" Their response is one of surprise to find out they did hurt you, because that was never their intent. Now that you realize this discrepancy, you begin the search for the breakdown that is preventing them from accomplishing their goal.

Once you determine that the problem is that they can't sense the amount of pressure being delivered, you start to view everyday situations differently. The slamming of the car door and refrigerator, that previously you may have thought to be behavioral choices, can now be accurately viewed as sensory issues.

Sensory—STAT Example 4.3

Step 1: Assess the situation

Joshua, Danny, and Michael were playing with their Star Wars light sabers, pretending to have a battle. From upstairs, I heard repeated cries of "Stop, Josh. Ow, Josh. Quit it Josh." I could tell the situation was escalating, as Joshua was not changing his behavior.

Step 2: Develop a hypothesis

Why? Why did they react the way they did? What could they be thinking? Select one or more of the elements below.

• Abstract language	• Motor	• Sensory	• Spatial orientation
• Control/ consistency	• Thinking about others thinking	• Social communication	• Emotions
• Mental flexibility	• Impulsive	• Executive function	• Anxiety

Hypothesis about their thinking (take a guess)

"I really like playing this game. I'm going to win. I'm having fun. Danny hit me as hard as I hit him, and it didn't hurt me." He doesn't realize how hard he is hitting.

Step 3 (optional): Ask questions to obtain a step-by-step account

Types of questions

"What's the problem?" "What's going on here?"

 Revise hypothesis. Go back to Step 2

Step 4: Actions to consider

Take action	Seek additional sources of help	• educators (teachers, aides, counselors, principal)
Take no action	• family members	• support professionals
Explain	• physician (change medication)	• parents of other children
Explain and take action	• neuropsychologist (further assessment)	• friends

First, I put a stop to the situation. Then, I explained to Danny and Michael that Joshua can't tell how hard he is hitting them. I explain to them that he doesn't understand what they want him to do when they tell him to stop, because he doesn't realize what he is doing wrong. Instead, they need to tell him, "Josh, you are hitting too hard and it is hurting me. Don't swing the light saber so hard."

In addition, I explain to Joshua that he needs to think and be aware of how hard he is hitting with the light saber. He needs to remember that he can't tell how hard he is hitting, so he really needs to listen to what his brothers are saying.

Finally, I give them a couple other options that may result in a happier outcome, i.e. pretend to hit in slow motion, or choreograph their moves like they do in the movies, so each of them knows what to expect.

Additional comments

As soon as I heard that the situation was not going well, I intervened in an effort to try to head off an all-out fight. There usually is a very small window in which to act before this happens. I really feel it's good for Joshua to interact with his brothers this way, as it gives us an opportunity to learn in a safer environment. However, once tempers flare, that opportunity not only is lost, but it doesn't present itself again for a while, as the other boys don't want to put themselves in that situation again any time soon.

Chapter 5

Spatial Orientation

"But I just barely touched him," Joshua insisted as Michael stood there with his tooth in his hand, blood covering his mouth.

"I was really aggravated that people kept bumping into me until I thought about where I was"—Leslie H-P while attending the NLD conference.

There we were, moving in opposite directions, making our way through the wide open, uncluttered room. There was never a thought that reaching my destination would be impeded by his presence. The situation seemed harmless when wham! I felt like I'd been hit with such force that it must have been a Mack truck, but no, it turned out to be a truck by the name of Joshua. In recovery mode, I turned and asked, "Why did you do that?" Joshua looked at me with a puzzled expression and innocently inquired as to what my problem was. It was then that I realized that not only did he not feel the force of the impact as painfully as I did, but he didn't have the ability to maneuver within this wide open space so as to avoid the contact. He was as shocked as I was that our plan to cross the room had been thwarted, but even more surprised to find out he was at fault. Situations of this type can and do occur in every environment.

As previously discussed, spatial orientation is intertwined with the motor and sensory areas. Because they are so interconnected, it is often difficult to distinguish which deficit area impacted the behavior being analyzed. Sometimes, all three affect the behavior. When hypothesizing about a child's behavior, it is not always necessary to be able to specifically determine which deficit area is responsible. As long as a parent or teacher is able to narrow it down to one or a combination, you will typically be able to make appropriate accommodations. So keep in mind as you read this chapter that the overlap of these three areas will be evident in the stories presented here. As with every deficit area, each child's ability with regards to spatial orientation will be different resulting in strengths and weaknesses that are unique to them.

As you think about the child with neurological differences, it's frightening to imagine maneuvering the world with a spatial orientation deficit. Even if this were your only deficit area, the world would be a scary place. Difficulties with spatial orientation cause the individual great confusion, making the simplest task seem insurmountable. Spatial orientation skills are those that allow us to navigate our path through the various environments we encounter daily, such as home, school, office, shopping malls, and restaurants. Getting there is only part of the battle because, once you arrive, each individual situation brings its own set of spatial requirements. Oftentimes well intended plans go awry with the implementation of the action. For example, many times at home children may simply want to pour themselves a drink of iced tea. They have the glass. They have the tea, but the two shall never meet.

The spatial orientation and motor areas often combine to make children with neurological differences appear uncoordinated and clumsy. As they walk through their environment they have a tendency to walk unawares into doorframes and bump into other people. Think about walking through the classrooms of today. Few classrooms have nice straight rows of desks. They have various work centers, tables, and desk groupings, each classroom layout being different depending on the teacher's purpose. These arrangements can present complications for children with spatial orientation difficulties. Hallways can also be a source of difficulty for them, especially if there are other children present. They can seem like a pinball bouncing off one person into another for the length of the hallway. Throw in a band instrument, and you have a recipe for disaster with the casualty count increasing with every step. I'll never forget, in sixth grade, the look of disbelief on the teacher's face in our beginning of the year meeting when I told her what to expect with Joshua and his brand new trombone. I explained, if left without support in getting to the band room, he would leave in his wake a group of unsuspecting and now wounded classmates, oblivious of them as he continued on. Plans were also made at that meeting for seating in the band room to accommodate his spatial orientation issues. Sitting in the front row or some other location where no one was in front of him would be necessary, for the safety of others as well as to reduce the need to hire an additional nurse. So far, so good, but next we have marching band to look forward to.

Walking in familiar environments, like home and school, creates problems to varying degrees for many children with neurological differences. Hard as it may be to believe, Grace would have trouble finding her way back to her seat after sharpening her pencil. Even when provided with this information, many educational teams have trouble believing it's a part of her disability. In fact, she simply forgets where she has been sitting. It was also difficult for Grace to find the most efficient way to navigate through the classroom. She would instead devise a path that a typical child would not ever think of taking, wreaking havoc along the way. I once heard a woman with Alzheimer's, whose name I unfortunately cannot remember, describe the devastation and panic she felt upon realizing she was lost in her own environment. "Here I am in my backyard. I can't remember how I got here or how to get back." This aptly describes the plight of children with neurological differences and makes one think how much more difficult life is when you have to overcome these obstacles.

If figuring out how to get from one location to the other in a familiar environment is a problem, think about trying to find your way around the larger, unfamiliar environments that we all encounter. Finding your car in a parking lot can be a difficult task for neurotypicals. For people with neurological disorders, it can be like finding a needle in a haystack. After speaking with an adult in this situation, it was interesting to discover her biggest criterion in purchasing a car was color. This in and of itself is not unusual; however, the reason for it is. Her main concern was finding the brightest, most eye-catching color in order to facilitate locating it in parking lots. Before requiring independence from these children, it is our obligation as caregivers and educators to consider their ability to travel through their world and remain safe both physically and emotionally.

Spatial orientation obstacles the children encounter occur not only when walking around, they also can be a problem when sitting down. Just the act of sitting down requires spatial orientation abilities. Many times Grace was not able to judge where her body was in relation to the chair. Consequently, she would catch only half of the chair on the way to the floor. Spatial orientation issues make it difficult for children with neurological differences to find their bodies in space. From a very young age, Joshua would participate in speech therapy sessions seated so close to Leslie H-P you would think they were attached. Although she would like to attribute this to his undying affection towards her, another possible consideration may be his need to find his body in space.

Dinnertime always has potential for being an adventure. Mealtimes require the constant movement of objects on the table in relation to one another. Food is brought to the table and removed from the table. You move your plate close to a serving dish to get a helping of food. You reach for seasonings and condiments. You pick up your glass, take a drink, and set it down, but where you set it down is the key. These are just a few examples, but all of them contribute to making mealtimes a spatial orientation jungle. So many times a simple attempt to obtain an item on the table has the same effect as one domino hitting another. One evening when sitting in an Italian restaurant, Joshua, at age twelve, spotted a breadstick he wanted. As I held my piece of pizza, poised to take a bite, Joshua quickly reached across the table, grabbing the breadstick. As he moved to get the breadstick to his mouth, I was suddenly met by an elbow cramming the hot piece of pizza into my face. If I had reacted in a typical manner with an angry comment, Joshua would have been totally surprised, as he had no idea he had done anything other than get a breadstick to eat. Once you know something is totally unintentional and oftentimes can't be helped, these types of occurrences are easier to view in a new light. The typical result would have been me scolding Joshua for his actions, him wondering what he had done now, with the final result being a further erosion of his self-esteem. All that upset would not have changed his future behavior in any way. Because I was able to attribute this incident to his spatial orientation deficit, I wasn't upset and we were able to continue on with a pleasant evening.

Pouring is also a task that requires sophisticated spatial orientation skills. Because everyone's goal is to have the child be independent and feel success, you look for opportunities to foster that. Whether making brownies or completing science experiments, pouring a liquid from one container to another often looks promising and so benign. Shortly after the pizza incident, Joshua wanted to make brownies. I thought I had set us up for success, as I had pre-measured out the ingredients. All that was required was pouring them into the target…a huge bowl. It all seemed simple enough. With a feeling of confidence, I turned to put something in the sink, assuming all was well. Next thing I hear is Joshua saying, "Um, I spilled a little water." Wanting to continue to make this a pleasant experience, I replied, "No problem," thinking it was in fact just a little water. As I went to clean it up, I realized it was all the water the brownies required. I still can't figure out how he missed that bowl.

The school setting presents the same spatial orientation challenges in a different environment. Pouring is necessary in science. Eating is required in the cafeteria, but nothing can match the skill required to balance a tray of food while weaving in and out of the crowd, and managing to place the tray in a specific spot on a table surrounded by classmates. In the classroom, spatial orientation is required to manage your supplies to make it through a day. Transferring books and supplies from your book bag to your locker, from the locker to the classroom, and in and out of your desk requires constant use of spatial skills. In second grade, Grace was required to return her pencil to a community pencil holder situated in the middle of a worktable. Each day her repeated attempts were unsuccessful and her pencil lay on the table. The teacher initially viewed this as defiant behavior but came to realize Grace did not have the ability to find the pencil holder.

Since writing is the most the common method teachers use to assess a student's knowledge, it can become a major area of concern for children with spatial difficulties. Writing and coloring in the margins, lining up the numbers on math worksheets, interpreting maps and graphs, and visually busy worksheets are all areas that present problems. Their ability to complete these tasks to meet a teacher's expectations often causes a negative effect on their grade, even though they may cognitively understand the material.

For most people, the visual spatial skills required to navigate an environment occur at an unconscious level and aren't even given a second thought. To have to bring this to a conscious level increases the cognitive load that may diminish the child's ability to perform another part of the task. Recently, I fell and hurt my back. Throughout the recuperation process, I had to constantly think about how to maneuver and position my body in an effort to alleviate pain. This experience caused me to realize that having to put so much cognitive energy into something that you normally take for granted is mentally exhausting and takes away from your quality of life. Children with neurological disorders are forced to expend this type of cognitive effort in every aspect of their day. When one stops to think about this, it brings to light how very courageous these children are, day after day.

Things to consider

- Familiarize children with the environments they will encounter and provide as much support as needed for them to remain safe:
  - practice routes they will need to take in various environments

- ○ mark routes with stickers on wall, tape on floor, point out or list landmarks
- ○ provide a buddy.
- Keep arrangement of the environment the same.
- Provide an organizational system at home and school—for example, label shelves, color-code binders.
- Allow additional time for moving from one location to another if necessary.
- When analyzing behavior, consider whether it can be attributed to the child's lack of ability to find their body in space.
- When accidents occur, consider their visual spatial ability to maneuver items.

Spatial orientation—STAT Example 5.1

Step 1: Assess the situation
In science class, Joshua was completing an experiment which required one drop of a chemical be put into a beaker. More than one drop would cause a different reaction. The aide immediately realized this would present a problem.

Step 2: Develop a hypothesis
Why? Why did they react the way they did? What could they be thinking? Select one or more of the elements below.

• Abstract language	• Motor	• Sensory	• Spatial orientation
• Control/ consistency	• Thinking about others thinking	• Social communication	• Emotions
• Mental flexibility	• Impulsive	• Executive function	• Anxiety

Hypothesis about their thinking (take a guess)

"I want to do this science experiment like everyone else. I can't wait to put the chemical in the beaker." The aide knew that it would be difficult for Joshua to determine how much pressure to use on the dropper, as well as achieve the physical act of getting it into the beaker.

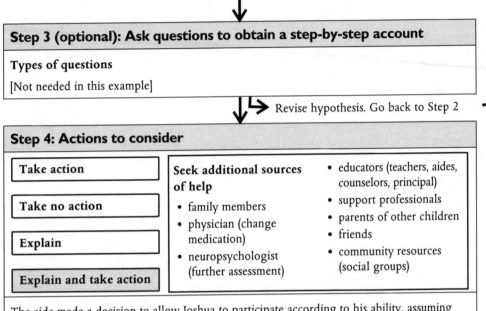

Step 3 (optional): Ask questions to obtain a step-by-step account

Types of questions

[Not needed in this example]

Revise hypothesis. Go back to Step 2

Step 4: Actions to consider

Take action

Take no action

Explain

Explain and take action

Seek additional sources of help

- family members
- physician (change medication)
- neuropsychologist (further assessment)

- educators (teachers, aides, counselors, principal)
- support professionals
- parents of other children
- friends
- community resources (social groups)

The aide made a decision to allow Joshua to participate according to his ability, assuming that if it didn't go as planned she would observe and use another student's results. She then told Joshua, "Squeeze it easy and just once," as she guided his hand and stabilized it over the beaker.

Additional comments

In an effort to maintain the child's self-esteem, it's important to allow them to participate to the extent that they can, while considering their safety and that of those around them. The self-esteem issue was, and should be, primary, knowing that the academic goal can be attained by other methods.

Chapter 6

Control/Consistency

Michael yells, "Come on Josh, we have to be home at 7:30." Joshua confidently replies, "It's only 7:27."

In fourth grade, Joshua's teacher sent a note home, which said, "Josh requested clarification today when we did not begin our oral reading at 9:45, but waited for children to complete assignments until 9:50. He certainly likes to keep us on schedule."

When one of your family members is diagnosed with a neurological difference, it quickly becomes evident that routine is essential. While all children benefit from some structure and routine, there is no question children with neurological differences cannot survive without them. Their neurological impairment makes them perceive the world in a different way than we do. It's not a wrong way; it's just a different way. Many times they're not sure what reaction they're going to get or what's going to happen next. Relying on rules and routines allows them to bring order to a world that they view as unpredictable. When you know what to expect, you have a greater chance of feeling safe. So often they might be perceived as bossy and controlling, when, in reality, they simply want to function in an environment that makes sense to them. Obviously this would account for their difficulty in transitioning and adapting to change. The impact of this is widespread, encompassing family, school, and social relationships.

Family members always try to adjust to the needs of one another with the ultimate goal being a happy, cohesive unit. Parents want each of their children to be happy, but if one of your children has a neurological difference their needs are often moved to the forefront. In an effort to minimize the potential for upset that would impact the entire family, their needs are addressed first. Sometimes this can be perceived by siblings as favoritism, when in fact, it's an attempt to manage the situation so the outcome can be positive for everyone. One Christmas when Joshua was ten, we made our usual trip to stay with relatives out of town. Each year in the past, we had all slept in one room with all three boys on the floor. This year the plans needed to change to accommodate Todd's brother's family. We knew of this change in advance, and I made the mistake of telling Joshua days earlier, which caused him great worry. My intent was to forewarn him of the change to give him time to adjust. Due to his level of anxiety, in hindsight I wish I had simply dealt with the change once we got there. For days leading up to the trip, he continued to interrogate me on the sleeping arrangements. Ultimately, to alleviate his fear, I told him I would sleep in the same room as him. Although Joshua was now completely satisfied, I understood I had created yet another problem with the other two boys. Sure enough, the other two boys were not happy to find out they would be excluded from what they considered to be our slumber party, due the number of beds available. Their disappointment was as real as Joshua's anxiety; however, I felt they were better able to deal with their issue than Joshua was with his. It's not uncommon for siblings to struggle with the circumstances that arrive daily, requiring the parent to make decisions that appear to be unfair to them.

Anytime you're away from home you are away from your routine and the safe and secure feelings it brings. Planning trips away from home cannot be done without taking the child's needs into account first. Grace's family rarely took a family vacation, but every few years they would think they had found a destination that Grace would truly enjoy. They had planned the dream cruise, one they were sure every child would love. At a family gathering that took place shortly after the cruise, everybody hopefully inquired as to the outcome, expecting rave reviews. The crowd was shocked to hear how miserable the trip had turned out. We heard horror stories about the food. In shock, we asked what the problem was. We were told that there was nothing on the cruise for Grace to eat except the occasional cheeseburger, but it was available only at certain times. Grace was not happy the entire trip. As a result, the family's memory of that cruise centers only on the food that was not available. Still, to this day, when the cruise is brought up, the only response is about the food, or rather lack thereof.

After years had passed, they decided to try another family vacation. This time they really thought they had ensured success because they asked Grace where *she* wanted to go. Being a history buff and having just read about Lake Placid, Grace decided she wanted to go there. They had planned to stay for a week, but returned home after a few days because Grace had decided she had seen enough. There was no sense in continuing with the trip, as Grace was seeing to it that they were as miserable as she was.

Families continuously, unconsciously adjust to the child's need for control and consistency in every arena. Many children with neurological differences develop intense areas of interest. They become immersed in a particular area, which allows them consistency and comfort. It's a world they create that allows predictability. Because there is so little they can control, they try to find something they can. Over the years, Joshua's area of interest has changed, starting with toy diecast racing cars (Nascars), moving on to monster trucks, then to game shows, *Star Wars*, and video games, and continues to evolve. One area of interest seems to lead to a new one. From about four until he was seven, Nascars were the word of the day. Because he was interested in Nascars and that made him happy, we naturally supported his interest, as families do for any child. During this time he amassed a hefty collection of cars housed in a special case. One day, as Joshua and I were walking up the steps to put his cars away, I inadvertently dropped the case and watched the hundred cars spill out down the steps. Joshua let out a cry of distress, which I calmly responded to by telling him, "Don't worry. It will be all right. Let's just put them back." That didn't work. He looked at me with tears in his eyes and said, "But, they were in order." Naïvely I continued on, not fully grasping the severity of the situation from his point of view. "Well, okay. What order were they in? Numerical order, by color?" This still didn't work. So I picked one up and asked him where it went. He took it from my hand and put it in a specific slot, fifth row down second from the right. I continued to do this with several additional cars, and it finally dawned on me that there was an order—one known only to him. Although I'm not sure what it was, because he could never put it into words, my guess is they were arranged in the case by the order in which they were received. At the time, I couldn't figure out why such a simple thing would be so upsetting to him. I now realize how this simple event took one of the only stable areas in his environment and threw it into chaos. In an instant, all the control that he had worked to achieve and that made him feel so comfortable was gone. Even if the area of interest is one that is age appropriate, it is the intensity with which they pursue it to the exclusion of other things that causes families to accommodate their need for consistency and control.

By age eleven, *Star Wars* was the all-consuming topic of Joshua's day. He would sit on the couch reading a *Star Wars* book while watching one of the movies. I remember being grateful that the six different episodes provided me variety, since I was going to have to listen to and watch them over and over again. Knowing of Joshua's *Star Wars* interest, his grandmother, Beverly, planned a trip to the children's science museum, where there was a *Star Wars* exhibit. On that day, grandma, grandpa, the three boys, and myself loaded into the car, anticipating a day the boys were sure to enjoy. This event was surely going to be the highlight of the summer for the boys. It was a can't miss…a surefire winner. On the way, I excitedly told Joshua that there was a *Star Wars* trivia contest that he could participate in. I was so ecstatic that all the time and energy and money spent on *Star Wars* was about to pay off in a big way. I had visions of a trophy and a cash prize that Joshua was sure to win. However, my enthusiasm was quickly replaced with shock, when he announced he had no intention of participating. That should have been my first indication that the day was not going to be as glorious as I had envisioned. As we entered the exhibit, it was obvious from the start that Joshua wanted no part of anything there that had to do with *Star Wars*. Joshua wasn't comfortable because he didn't know what to expect, and as a result he made sure our time spent there was miserable for one and all, until we relented and left. Family members who love the child automatically assume that anything having to do with their special interest will bring them joy. This is a perfect example that this is not the case. The joy comes from their ability to use their area of interest to exercise control over their world, and from the comfort they find in that consistency.

Consistency and control are important in any environment, and that includes school. Each school day is made up of one transition after the other. The more predictable the day can be, the easier it is for the child to make it through the day successfully. Neurotypical children find comfort in knowing the planned happenings for the day, just as children with neurological differences do. The difference is that children with neurological impairments only feel safe knowing every aspect of the schedule. The various aspects of the disorder make their ability to adjust to change an impossibility at times. Their neurotypical peers have a greater ability to go with the flow and make adjustments as needed. Parents know how critical it is on that first day of school for their child with neurological differences to be familiar with the schedule, as well as having one in hand to follow. Not knowing about the substitute teacher, changes in the lunch menu, indoor vs. outdoor recess, and schedule changes due to late arrivals/early dismissals, can quickly send them into a downhill spiral.

Staying on the schedule to the minute can be an issue for some, like Grace. If the class was scheduled to end at 11:30, she felt like it was her duty to notify the teacher by yelling out, "It's 11:31, we need to go to our next class." Obviously not all teachers find this type of information as helpful as it is intended. Somewhere Grace must have been thinking to herself, "I'm always supposed to follow the rules. I'm trying to help you follow the rules. I'm doing a good thing." Their attempt to be helpful, albeit well intentioned, often receives a negative response that leaves them confused as to what they did wrong.

The idea of following the rules to the letter does not always win friends. Take, for instance, the day Grace saw two girls her own age standing in an off-limits area. She quickly proceeded to notify them in an authoritative tone that they were not allowed to be there and needed to move. Needless to say, her advice was not taken as a friendly suggestion. In her mind, it was as simple as "Rules are meant to be followed; you're not following them, so it's my duty to tell you." This often carried over to the classroom, where her technique was just as effective, or ineffective, as the case may be. As the teacher gave directives to her class, such as "Boys clean this area up," Grace would feel compelled to restate the command to the boys in a teacher tone. Again, her good intentions met with discontent.

Many times these children try to control a situation in an effort to effectively participate. Knowing what comes next allows them to engage in social exchanges that would otherwise be risky due to the unpredictability. Joshua would often put himself in a position of referee or scorekeeper in an attempt to interact in a safe way. At indoor recess, Joshua approached two classmates playing checkers and told them he wanted to be the scorekeeper. One of the children replied, "There is no scorekeeper in checkers," in a condescending tone. Fortunately for Joshua, his classmate, Mason, who was aware of his diagnosis, supportively stated, "Just let him do it. It's not hurting anything." Because positive social interactions are few and far between, this kind intervention allowed Joshua to participate in a social event in a predictable way. For Joshua to be able to experience even one positive social event makes it a good day.

Making social situations work at home, school, or in the neighborhood is always a challenge, because the social situations the child encounters change the social rules they need to follow. If there were only one set of rules, they could follow them perfectly every time. When Joshua was at the end of third grade, he would have friends over and his social deficiencies became readily apparent. For example, he would invite Nick over because he truly enjoyed spending time with him and wanted to be his friend. His actions, even to a nine-year-old, weren't consistent with what he was trying to accomplish. Joshua would get himself a snack while Nick watched, waiting for an invitation that never came. He would play video games, thinking that Nick enjoyed watching him, and never once thought to ask Nick what he would like to do. Nick would leave the room or head for home and Joshua would never realize he was gone. After discussing what a disaster these attempts at friendship had become, I was worried he would push away the possibility of building any lasting friendships. We decided to use his need for structure to our advantage by developing a list of guidelines for him to follow when friends were invited over. The guidelines we developed were general enough to be used any time any friend came over, yet specific enough to guide him through the sequence of events that occur every time you have an invited guest. They were as simple as: greet the person at the door, ask them what they want to play (it has to be an activity for two people), when you get something to drink or eat ask them if they want something, walk them to the door and say goodbye when they leave. We wrote the rules down and reviewed them right before any friend was to come over. For Joshua, this framework was one that he could understand, use, and make work in a short amount of time. It proved to be golden in that it addressed so many problem areas quickly. The consistency of a simple list of rules allowed him to feel more in control and made all of his future interactions with visiting friends so much more positive. It's important to be careful to present things as "rules" only in circumstances that have little to no variability. In this example, you always greet a friend at the door; however, how you greet them depends on many variables. The more consistency and control in various situations that you can provide, the greater their chance of success.

Just as you can use routine to your advantage, it can also lead to consistent *un*wanted behavior. Parents need to be constantly aware that patterns can easily turn into routines. Once it becomes a routine for these children, it's much harder to change. For them, the routine is the routine, and that's the way it is and the way it's going to stay. This happened in our world and before I realized it, the damage was done. In our van, Joshua was the self-appointed keeper of the remote control of the DVD player. This was no surprise, given his need to control every situation possible. At that time, the younger two boys were at ages where they weren't interested in using the remote. They were happy to watch whatever was on. However, as they grew, they also wanted some input in determining what would be watched. By this time, the king of the remote was not willing to abdicate control, and fighting ensued. The problem was that it had become such a pattern that Joshua truly believed there was no other alternative than for him to be in control. Rectifying the situation proved to be exhausting.

Children diagnosed with neurological differences often rely on time for control and consistency to give order to their environment. Whether in school or social settings, their reliance on time can make them appear rigid to others. In third grade, when Joshua was spending the night with Nick, he suddenly got up to leave the room in the middle of playing. Nick asked him where he was going. Joshua replied to what he considered to be a ridiculous question, in a matter-of-fact tone, "I'm going to bed. It's nine o'clock." As if to say, the rule is, I go to bed at nine o'clock every night, no matter where I am or what I'm doing. Because Jane, Nick's mom, relayed that story to me, it impressed upon me the need to always consider the circumstances beforehand and attempt to explain changes Joshua may encounter that differ from his normal routine. In this case, it would have been as simple as saying, "When you spend the night at a friend's, you usually stay up later than your normal bedtime and that's okay." This is a constant consideration that parents need to keep in mind for each new situation, but it's not always easy to anticipate possible problem areas. So many things that never need to be explained to a neurotypical child need to be explained to children with neurological disorders in order to provide the control and consistency that they need in order to succeed.

Because control and consistency are vital to helping these children make sense of their world, it is important to think about changes before they are made. Change is inevitable. Frequently, decisions can be made about how change is handled that can lessen its potentially negative impact on the child and those around them. One should consider whether the change is necessary, what impact it will have and on whom, and is it important enough to warrant the upset. Routines and consistency allow these children the control they need to function. When you analyze their behavior, think about how it is affected by their control, or lack of it. It can make the difference between viewing a behavior as intentionally negative, or as an attempt to maintain order. It can sometimes be beneficial to use the child's reliance on routines and consistency to everyone's advantage. In order to do this, it's imperative to keep it in the forefront of your thinking as they enter each situation that will be new to them.

Things to consider

- Provide a schedule and have a routine.
- Explain changes in the schedule or routine that you are aware of ahead of time.
- Pick your battles.
- Consider whether you want a behavior to become a routine.
- Give in-depth explanations.
- Tell the child what to do instead.
- Consider how much support is needed to help them enter new situations.

Control/consistency—STAT Example 6.1

Step 1: Assess the situation

In fourth grade, the teacher sent a note home saying "Joshua held back a girl and would not let her through because she was running."

Step 2: Develop a hypothesis

Why? Why did they react the way they did? What could they be thinking? Select one or more of the elements below.

• Abstract language	• Motor	• Sensory	• Spatial orientation
• Control/ consistency	• Thinking about others thinking	• Social communication	• Emotions
• Mental flexibility	• Impulsive	• Executive function	• Anxiety

Hypothesis about their thinking (take a guess)

"I want to be first in line. You're trying to get in front of me."

Step 3 (optional): Ask questions to obtain a step-by-step account

Types of questions

"Why did you hold her back?" He replied, **"Because she was running, and that is against the rules."**

↓ ↳ Revise hypothesis. Go back to Step 2

Step 2: Develop a hypothesis

Why? Why did they react the way they did? What could they be thinking? Select one or more of the elements below.

• Abstract language	• Motor	• Sensory	• Spatial orientation
• Control/ consistency	• Thinking about others thinking	• Social communication	• Emotions
• Mental flexibility	• Impulsive	• Executive function	• Anxiety

Hypothesis about their thinking (take a guess)

"She wasn't following the rules, so I needed to stop her. The rules must be followed."

↓

Step 4: Actions to consider

Take action	**Seek additional sources of help**	• educators (teachers, aides, counselors, principal)
Take no action	• family members	• support professionals
Explain	• physician (change medication)	• parents of other children
		• friends
Explain and take action	• neuropsychologist (further assessment)	• community resources (social groups)

I explained to Joshua that it is not his job to enforce the rules with other students. That is the teacher's job.

Additional comments

After taking a guess, I asked follow-up questions to confirm. While Joshua's answers confirmed that I had accurately selected the correct deficit area, his response enabled me to provide an explanation to address his thinking specifically.

In so many circumstances like this that involve other students, it could prove to be extremely helpful to provide explanations to the neurotypical peer about why the child with the neurological difference did what they did. In this case the girl involved could have been told that Joshua did not intend to be mean, but was trying to prevent her from getting in trouble because she was breaking the rules. So often these explanations do not occur, leaving the neurotypical peer a negative lasting impression of the child, and so reducing the possibility for a potential friendship.

Control/consistency—STAT Example 6.2

Step 1: Assess the situation
Because Joshua loved video games, the family decided to go to an attraction in Orlando that housed many opportunities that revolved around virtual reality and video games. This was the first time we had been there, but were sure all the kids would love it. Riding over in the car, Joshua began to complain how awful this was going to be. Once inside, Joshua threw a fit about trying anything, saying he was sure he wouldn't like it. This continued until we left, even though some of the games there were the same ones he played at home and enjoyed. He proceeded to make this outing unbearable for everyone. A year later, he wanted to go back.

↓

Step 2: Develop a hypothesis

Why? Why did they react the way they did? What could they be thinking? Select one or more of the elements below.

• Abstract language	• Motor	• Sensory	• Spatial orientation
• Control/ consistency	• Thinking about others thinking	• Social communication	• Emotions
• Mental flexibility	• Impulsive	• Executive function	• Anxiety

Hypothesis about their thinking (take a guess)

"This is too noisy and loud. These lights are bothering me. This is overwhelming."

↓

Step 3 (optional): Ask questions to obtain a step-by-step account

Types of questions

When Joshua expressed his desire to go back a year later, it caused me to reassess my original hypothesis. "So," I asked Joshua, "if you didn't like it the first time, why do you want to go back?" He said, "**Because I like the games they had.**"

↳ Revise hypothesis. Go back to Step 2

Step 2: Develop a hypothesis

Why? Why did they react the way they did? What could they be thinking? Select one or more of the element below.

• Abstract language	• Motor	• Sensory	• Spatial orientation
• Control/ consistency	• Thinking about others thinking	• Social communication	• Emotions
• Mental flexibility	• Impulsive	• Executive function	• Anxiety

Hypothesis about their thinking (take a guess)

"*When I was there the first time, it was all too new. I didn't know what to expect.*"

Step 4: Actions to consider

Take action

Take no action

Explain

Explain and take action

Seek additional sources of help

- family members
- physician (change medication)
- neuropsychologist (further assessment)

- educators (teachers, aides, counselors, principal)
- support professionals
- parents of other children
- friends
- community resources (social groups)

Because we had spent so much money to get in, we kept trying to find a way for Joshua to enjoy himself, but finally had to give in by cutting our visit short and going home.

Additional comments

Although I still believe there was a sensory component involved, due to Joshua's later comments about wanting to return, it caused me to question my initial hypothesis, which assumed the cause was totally sensory. Now, even though sensory may have been a contributing factor, I think the overriding issue was that the situation placed him in an environment where he felt unsure because of the unfamiliar surroundings. Due to the extent of his upset, he was unable to overcome his anxiety and fear enough to even consider enjoying any aspect of the event. As the family has talked about it since, Joshua has changed his thinking about going back because he now knows what to expect, and has had time to process the environment while absent from it.

Chapter 7

Thinking about Others Thinking (Theory of Mind)

"If someone breaks in, I hope they don't steal my monster truck collection"—Joshua.

Thinking about what others are thinking, sometimes referred to as "theory of mind," is without a doubt one of the most important abilities human beings possess. It is necessary to successfully navigate the world—however, as with so many other abilities, some people are more adept than others. It absolutely impacts every social interaction we encounter and almost every decision we make. The capability to think about what someone else is thinking involves one's ability to take another's perspective, but it is so much more. It encompasses one's capacity to empathize, encourage, console, apologize, compliment, determine motive and intent, detect deception, lie, persuade others, compromise, negotiate, share, feel embarrassed, and even ask for help. The minute someone enters your environment, you automatically begin to determine what actions you will take in relation to what that person will think. Whether you are in your home, or in a public place, you automatically consider the thinking of others. It's such a natural, unconscious part of the thought process, like a reflex. You don't ever have to think about it; the ability is just there. When it's not there, the impact is far-reaching.

Our ability to think about others thinking affects every relationship we experience, from the most insignificant to the most meaningful. It's what advertising and sales are all about. Whether consciously or unconsciously, all relationships are built on the basis of mutual benefit. Human beings are always thinking about what the other person is thinking. Think for a moment about ordering in a fast food restaurant. It's a brief exchange that most probably will not result in any lasting relationship. From the time you give the person your order to the time you get your food, you consider their disposition, how much information they need, and whether they simply want your order or want to exchange pleasantries. As a result of your assessment, you determine what action you will take and the manner in which that will be presented. The same thinking also applies to more meaningful, long-lasting relationships, such as those among family members. Every parent deals with trying to get their children to comply with their wishes—for instance, the evening ritual of getting your children ready for bed. In my house, it can go one of two ways. I can say, "Go upstairs and get ready for bed." Sometimes I say it once, and sometimes I have to say it five, ten, or what seems to be fifteen times with increasing volume. When I determine that my children might respond more promptly with a little enticement, then I might say, "Let's see who can get their pajamas on the fastest." It's all in an attempt to change their thinking from "This is a job" to "This is a game." To quote my middle son, Danny, "Give the people what they think they want, so you can get what you want." That so eloquently sums up theory of mind.

If I were given a magic wand and allowed to fix one deficit area in an effort to improve Joshua's life, there is no question I would select the ability to think about others thinking. The effects of a deficit in this area are incredibly far-reaching. This may be best illustrated by looking at the Systematic Tool to Analyze Thinking (STAT). The ability to think about others thinking directly interrelates with an individual's ability to function effectively in the areas of social communication, language, emotions, executive functioning (problem-solving), impulsivity, and ultimately anxiety. Theory of mind is the major building block that most contributes to the development of all these areas. It is the successful combination of all of these areas that allows us to foster meaningful relationships, and life is about meaningful relationships.

In trying to understand the impact this deficit has on children diagnosed with neurological differences, you must make a conscious effort to think like them…as if you are mindblind and *can't* think about what someone else is thinking. It can often be the key that gives you the insight that you need to understand why the children act as they do. In the process of trying to think through Joshua's behavior, theory of mind was one of the many deficit areas we considered. Over time, as we honed our skills in thinking in a mindblind way, we realized the pervasive nature of theory of mind. We then began to view it as fundamental in many of the situations we tried to analyze. From that point on, the analysis became easier.

Developing the skill to think as if you are mindblind is difficult, because it goes against your natural instinct. Learning to think in this way is a long, arduous process. Parents begin asking their children at a very young age to think about the other person in order to train them to be socially successful. On every playground and in every home, parents can be heard asking their children, "Would you like that if someone did that to you?" When raising children with neurological differences, this question is asked much more frequently, and over a much longer period of time. Joshua is now in seventh grade and I've asked him, and continue to ask him, this question more times than I care to remember. His response is always, "No, I wouldn't." With neurotypical children, the discussion stops there because the child *is* able to understand how the other person feels and realize they shouldn't do it again. However, with Joshua, I have to continue with the next logical question of, "Well then, why did you do it?" He responds with, "I don't know," or a blank stare. After this typical exchange, it's obvious to me that Joshua is unable to make the intended connection that most children so easily make, "If you don't like it, don't do it to somebody else." I'm obviously asking him to do something he's not capable of doing. It doesn't mean I should stop trying. It simply means I need to be cognizant of this and continue to try to get through with more detailed explanations and meaningful examples.

Once you begin to think this way, you can begin to understand the enormous effect this deficit has. In our experience, trying to explain the impact of mindblindness has been met with the most resistance. It seems to be the hardest area for people who do not understand children with neurological differences to grasp. First of all, it's hard enough for you to understand. Then to try to convince school personnel, family members, or other community members, such as troop leaders, other parents, or coaches can often be a fruitless endeavor. So often you feel under pressure to offer an explanation for a complicated subject in a very short amount of time. You're lucky if you get five minutes. Theory of mind is such an intricate part of the human condition, it's hard to fathom life without it, but once you try, it goes a long way to explaining the thinking of children with neurological differences.

Those of us who have theory of mind abilities can look at a situation from various points of view. As we present scenarios from home and school, we hope to illustrate successfully how difficult it can be for all parties involved when someone can't think about how someone else is thinking. Children with theory of mind deficits have no concept that others think anything different than they think. They assume their knowledge base is everyone's knowledge base. Up until fifth grade, Joshua thought that anything that he knew, I knew. As a result, he never felt the need to share any information about his day, always assuming that I knew what had occurred. Each day when he came home, I had to continually prod him with questions and prompt him with choices of possible answers. This would continue on well into the evening, often with no result. This made it particularly difficult to get the necessary details whenever Joshua appeared to be upset about something. The effects carried over into every aspect of his life. I would listen in on his brief, social phone calls, which were few and far between, so that I would know the times and dates scheduled for any social happenings. In addition, any book that Joshua read, I read as well, so that I would know what he was talking about, or could explain behaviors he would take on. A typical conversation would begin with my questioning why he was doing something and he would respond with, "You know, like in that book…" with the assumption that I always did know. To this day Joshua, at the age of twelve, honestly continues to believe that I find great joy in watching him play video games. The thought never enters his mind that I might have other things around the house that would consume my time.

Taking theory of mind into account has made me rethink some typical societal responses. Each night in many American homes, mothers tell their children, "I love you," with the typical response being, "I love you too, Mom." Now let me tell how it goes in my house. I say, "I love you," and a sweet little voice replies, "I know." The first time I heard this it caused me to stop and ponder this unusual, apparently self-absorbed, response. Upon further reflection, I've decided his response is totally appropriate, because my purpose in telling him was so that he would know. He acknowledged that, and nothing more was needed. I'm starting to worry about myself because his thinking is starting to make perfect sense to me! If you really think about it, if you tell someone you love him or her with the sole purpose of hearing back, "I love you too," then the question you should really be asking is, "Do you love me?" Although I've come to understand this, you probably shouldn't try it at home.

Obviously, the theory of mind deficit impacts interpersonal relationships in the home. One Saturday morning as I sat peacefully reading the paper, I was rudely interrupted by a flying pear that hit me on the side of my head. As I recovered from the blow, I turned to see a ten-year-old Joshua looking at me, wondering why I didn't catch it. Because it hurt, I initially felt just a tad of anger… That may be an understatement. I asked him why he would feel the need to throw a pear at my head. He innocently said, "I wanted you to cut it up." I again questioned, "So you threw it at my head?" And then came the telling response, "No, I wanted you to catch it the way you did yesterday when I threw it to you." This response changed my thinking about the whole event. I was no longer mad because I realized he didn't understand that we both needed to be thinking in the same way. I remember telling him, "You need to make sure I'm looking at you and that I know what you are going to do before you throw it. Next time say, 'Mom, heads up,' then I will know you are going to throw something to me." Let me just say now, when I hear, "Mom, heads up," my body is automatically in a state of alert.

Needless to say, compromise has continually been a point of emphasis over the years. One of Joshua's weekly assignments from Leslie H-P had been to compromise once a day. I sent Joshua and Danny out to get the garbage can and Joshua came back into the house and proudly exclaimed, "Mom we compromised." Danny was quick to interject, "It's not compromising when you *demand* I take the can and you take the lid, which is the easiest thing to carry." It was clear there was more work to be done.

In our home, Joshua often appears to be cold and uncaring, in his brothers' eyes. This has been, and continues to be, a recurring concern in our home. Danny and Michael understandably have an extremely difficult time understanding Joshua's thinking. When you can't share, compromise, or negotiate, it's hard to build loving relationships. Therefore, there wasn't a lack of material when choosing stories to illustrate this. The following story stands out as one I want to share, because it illustrates how desperate I was to have Joshua understand theory of mind, even before I knew that it existed.

Like all parents, I tried to teach Joshua to share by asking, for example, "How would you feel if they had something you wanted to play with?" When he answered, "They don't," I realized I needed to plan a situation where he would. By the time Joshua was in third grade, he had accumulated a decent size monster truck collection that no one was allowed to touch or disturb in any way. I purchased two monster trucks as a gift for Danny, so that Joshua would be forced to ask Danny to share them with him. Like so many other plans, it didn't quite fulfil my expectations. I was accurate in assuming he would want to play with the trucks, but that was the only thing I was right about. Instead of asking to play with them, he assumed, because they were monster trucks and his domain, that he was entitled to play with them whenever he chose, without ever asking Danny. This, of course, made Danny upset and angry, which led to a constant battle whenever Joshua wanted to play with them. Joshua was never able to get the point about how it feels when someone chooses not to share with you, or consequently generalize it so as to be able to understand how he makes others feel when he refuses to share.

Sometimes you do not feel or see the progress that is being made. It happens in small, incremental steps, but it happens. It can be helpful to look back over larger time-frames of maybe one or two years to help you gain perspective on how far the child has come. One recent situation occurred at our house when Michael came running into the house in tears, screaming. Through his sobs, I was able to decipher that he had lost his $35 video game that he had just purchased with his own, hard-earned money that morning. What made this seem to be particularly hopeless was that this video game was somewhere in the vast outdoors where he had been playing—and measured only one inch by one inch in size. It was quickly getting dark, which added to the urgency. Danny, Michael, and I immediately went outside to begin a search. Unaware, Joshua eventually made his way out and asked what was going on. Danny told him, "Michael had lost his game," so Joshua began to help in the search. Joshua's actions showed empathy for Michael's plight. This in and of itself was progress and lasted for about all of ten minutes, but I was happy making a mental note to praise him later. The three of us continued to look after Joshua went back into the house. Eventually, we found the game and triumphantly entered the house, pleased with our success. Joshua excitedly asked if we found it. We told him we did and he replied in a heartfelt tone, "Oh, good!" This was a great moment, everyone was happy, and Joshua's empathy was even more apparent. The feeling of accomplishment on all fronts was short-lived. The words had just left Joshua's mouth when Michael countered, "Like you care. You hardly even helped us look!" Because Danny never quit looking, Michael discounted Joshua's show of empathy. Danny's empathetic reaction to the crisis was so much more pronounced, highlighting the stark contrast. This was the start of yet another long round of explanations. For Michael, this meant the explanation that Joshua really did show that he cared, and that those actions needed to be encouraged if we wanted to see more of them. For Joshua, I wanted to be sure he understood that what he did and said had shown us that he cared.

Having a child who is mindblind can sometimes have advantages for parents. The child's inability to lie makes it easier to sort out who is at fault when there are other siblings or peers involved. Many times in our house we would have a line-up in order to interrogate the boys on who was responsible for a certain action or mishap. We always started with Joshua because we knew the process could stop there, or possibilities would be immediately pared down. It would only take one question, "Did you do it?" If Joshua said "yes" that was the end of it, if he said "no" we were down to two. However, at school, this technique was ineffective because teachers could never believe that a child that old was incapable of lying. It probably wasn't until fifth grade that he began to attempt to lie, and has progressed nicely since then.

School is always an adventure when the child lacks the ability to think about someone else's thinking and school personnel find it difficult to understand or believe. The behavior of children who are mindblind is often misinterpreted as selfish, self-absorbed, disrespectful, and defiant. In fourth grade, a recurring concern expressed by Joshua's teacher was that he continued to read as a fellow student presented for the class, even getting up to choose another book from the bookshelf. Knowing that Joshua has the ability to read and listen at the same time with remarkable accuracy, I realized that he believed he was doing what was expected of him—listening to the presentation. When I asked him, "Did you know that reading your book while she was presenting hurt her feelings?" "No, why?" he responded. "Because it looks like you're not listening to her and you don't care what she has to say." "But, I *was* listening," Joshua explained, not understanding that she wouldn't know this based on his actions. It was clear that Joshua was not able to understand how others would view his actions. He was unable to think about what they might be thinking about him. His intent was never to be disrespectful or unkind; however, this affected not only the way the teacher viewed him, but the way his classmates did as well.

These negative labels gain reinforcement as situations arise where the child would normally be expected to help, compliment, or encourage others. Working in a group is typically a problem for children with neurological differences, because it requires all members to use their theory of mind skills. Many theory of mind skills are needed to be a successful team member, with compromising and negotiating being among the most prominent. In sixth grade, Joshua was part of a group in science, and each student in the group was assigned a task to perform. Joshua was not happy with the way the others were performing their duties and made it known to everyone, without concern for what they might think. Each time he is assigned to a group, problems arise.

There is no question that the impact of theory of mind deficits on academic performance is extensive. In second grade, every week Joshua had to write a paragraph to respond to a different writing prompt. The prompts that were the most difficult were those that required him to view the world from different points of view, such as "If you woke up and you were green, tell about your day" or "If you were a bird, describe what you would see as you flew around." His answers were always quite clear and to the point and went something like "I would go to the doctor," "I'm not a bird," or "How would I know?" Prompts such as these require pretending and imagination, which require the ability to think about others thinking.

It seems that third grade is the time when each student is required to give an oral report on a topic of their choosing. Neurotypical children approach this event with much trepidation and upset stomachs. However, for many children lacking theory of mind abilities, this event is a shining moment in their school history because they typically give the best presentation. Why? When you can't think about what the rest of the class is thinking, you are not nervous or embarrassed, and your performance can be given without having to navigate these problems. Teachers always seem so surprised and almost shocked at how well the child has done, because their presentation so far surpasses those of their peers. Unfortunately, this euphoric moment is a fleeting one for parents and their children in the course of their school career.

A theory of mind deficit may not be as apparent in the early grades but becomes an increasingly significant issue in the later grades. As the children get older, more emphasis is placed on author's purpose, point of view, mood, theme, persuasion, and writing to a specific audience, to name a few. At the beginning of each school year we tried to outline the academic areas that were affected by having a theory of mind deficit. Even with this information, Joshua's sixth grade teacher attributed his sudden decline in grades from A's to F's to a lack of effort, when in reality the problem was the questions being asked. The academic emphasis at that time was author's purpose and point of view. The effort was there in Joshua's response, but theory of mind wasn't.

Yet another example took place for Joshua in fifth grade math. As we worked through a "show your work" math problem, I would stop Joshua along the way and ask him how he got the answer, thinking he could then write that down in explanation of his thinking. Each step of the way he answered, "I put the numbers in the calculator." When I told him that he had to write down why he picked those numbers in order to explain his thinking, so the teacher would know he understood, he said, "Won't he know I understand it when I write the right answer down?"

The ability to think about someone else's thinking affects the way you react in social situations. Someone's aptitude at using developed social skills is dependent on the degree to which they have theory of mind. Early on we can observe the development of social skills in pretend play. Even as early as pre-school, children are expected to engage in pretend play, but without theory of mind, this is impossible. Since Joshua was our first child, we excitedly purchased toys that would develop his imagination, like action figures, western town playsets, farms, and cities. We were sure this would lead to hours of fun, but all it led to was hours of me picking up dumped toys.

Joshua did enjoy playing with cars, but not in an imaginative way. He would line up his cars, make indentations in the rug, and proceed to systematically run each car, one by one, over the pattern. This interest continued into third grade. Joshua and Nick would set up dual tracks in which to race their cars against each other. Joshua had amassed quite a collection, that no one was allowed to touch. Prior to Nick coming over for the big race, Joshua would proceed to remove any cars that Nick would have to choose from, that would have the possibility of beating him. He was assured a win. When I finally realized Nick was going home a loser every time, I began to worry that he might never want to come back. I tried to explain to Joshua, "You have to make sure Nick has fun when he's here, so he wants to come back. He won't have fun if he loses every time. So you and Nick need to take turns picking from all the cars so each of you can win sometimes." He never would agree to do this on his own. I had to insist that he do it that way, but it never really did work. He just could not understand this, and even now at twelve it can still be an issue. Even though he makes incremental progress, losing at anything is still very hard for him. He is unable to see the benefit of someone else winning, which makes family game night extremely stressful.

Having theory of mind is a prerequisite for determining someone else's intent. As you go through your day, you make judgements about the intent of others. If you think someone has made an honest mistake or accidentally done something, you will react differently than if you feel they have done it on purpose. During the fall of Joshua's fourth grade year, the extent to which Joshua's inability to understand intent, and to which that negatively impacted his life, was made apparent to Leslie H-P as I shared with her a scenario that had just taken place. Joshua was playing with a number of neighbor children on a trampoline. Joshua and a boy were jumping at the same time and the boy accidentally kicked Joshua in the face. Joshua immediately became enraged, and pinned the boy down, punching him, until an adult intervened. As with many incidents, the effect is felt by the entire family. In this case, Danny came in and asked me, "Oh, Mommy, how are we going to help him?" Even to a sibling two years his junior, Joshua's inability to handle a typical situation seemed obvious and extreme.

It's not only about someone else's intent; it's about how their intent is perceived by others and the effect that has on developing friendships. Joshua became a frequent visitor at a neighbor's house once he knew they had a video game system that he didn't. One night when he returned home after playing there, he asked me to explain what it meant when the boys had said he was using them for their game system. I told him they felt the only reason he was coming over was to play their game, not to spend time with them. He acknowledged what I said, but didn't seem to have any concept of hurting their feelings or what that might mean. His only real concern was how that would affect his future visits to play their video games.

Progress seems slow and incremental, but there is progress. I was so happy when Joshua came home from attending the book fair at school of his fourth grade year and proudly announced he had purchased gifts for his grandparents. He had never before taken the initiative to purchase gifts for anyone. Joy filled my heart. I couldn't wait to see what he had purchased. You could almost hear the drum roll as he reached into his backpack. The first book he presented was for Grandpa, and I was excited to see a Tiger Woods golf book, thinking he nailed it. Upon closer inspection, I saw it was a Tiger Woods golf book for children. I was still able to take some delight in his selection, because at least he was on the right track. It came to an abrupt halt when he pulled out Grandma's gift book, which was *The Hardy Boys*. I was sure she was just going to be ecstatic when she saw it. Although he didn't pick appropriate gifts, the progress was evident in that he had thought about giving a gift to someone else, which included what it would be and how it would make them feel. It may not have been perfect, but it showed great progress. Being the wonderful grandparents they are, they accepted their gifts with great fanfare and encouragement in an attempt to foster Joshua's future efforts.

Those of us with developed theory of mind capabilities understand that others have mental states different from our own. As a result, we know that others have differing beliefs, thoughts, desires, intentions, and can imagine things that we can't. Our discussions and conversations with others include the verbiage that denotes these mental states, such as, "in my opinion," "I believe," and "I think." When you are mindblind, however, you don't have those mental state verbs at your disposal because you don't understand there is a mental state other than the one you have. Take, for example, a situation Joshua encountered at school in sixth grade. A group of boys were discussing playing mature (M rated) video games intended for ages over eighteen. Joshua was part of this conversation and adamantly stated to his same-age peers that "It is not appropriate for children our age to play M rated games." As far as he was concerned, that was the end of the discussion because no one would, should, or could think anything else. His mindblindness denies him the ability to agree to disagree. His insistence in pursuing this definitely worked against him socially.

Relationships continue to be strained because typically these children may not apologize or say "please" and "thank you" because they don't understand the reasoning behind social pleasantries. Children who can't think about others thinking take the last roll in the basket, don't help others pick something up if they've dropped it, and close the door without a thought that someone might be following close behind. These actions are not carried out with any malicious intent, yet to the observing world they are viewed as a product of bad parenting. So often, before they get a diagnosis and develop a clear understanding of theory of mind, many parents question themselves and their ability to parent. It takes a long time to understand how vast the impact is, how different it makes the children look, causing them to stick out, and giving them the appearance of being self-absorbed. Even everyday activities intended for relaxation are influenced. The depth to which you are able to understand jokes, movies, and books will vary with your theory of mind capabilities. Thinking about others thinking is a skill that impacts your quality of life and is often taken for granted. You can't appreciate what a gift it is until you have to watch someone you love struggle to attempt to survive in the world without it.

Things to consider

- Only asking "How would you feel if that were you?" is not enough.

- Explain, explain, and explain again in different ways and in different situations.

- Involve the child in selecting gifts or cards for people, and discuss why that item might be appropriate for that person.

- Discuss what other people might be thinking, as you read a book together, watch a movie, and observe people when you're out in public.

- Look at commercials, advertisements, and talk about what they are trying to get you to think.

- Give the child small jobs that require them to think about the needs of others, such as feed a pet, walk the dog, water plants, help grandparents.

- Remember, progress is slow. Take joy in the progress you see, knowing you are heading in the right direction.

- Remember, it's not a reflection of parenting skills, but part of the disorder.

Thinking about others thinking—STAT Example 7.1

Step 1: Assess the situation
The teacher called home and said Joshua was broadcasting the fact that he could not get a detention to the other students. (Accommodations had in fact been made on Joshua's IEP to exclude him from detention.)

↓

Step 2: Develop a hypothesis

Why? Why did they react the way they did? What could they be thinking? Select one or more of the elements below.

• Abstract language	• Motor	• Sensory	• Spatial orientation
• Control/ consistency	• Thinking about others thinking	• Social communication	• Emotions
• Mental flexibility	• Impulsive	• Executive function	• Anxiety

Hypothesis about their thinking (take a guess)

"It's true. I don't have to go to detention. I don't see any reason not to tell you. I'm simply answering the question you asked of me."

↓

Step 3 (optional): Ask questions to obtain a step-by-step account
Types of questions
[Not needed in this example]

↓ ↳ Revise hypothesis. Go back to Step 2

Step 4: Actions to consider		
Take action Take no action Explain Explain and take action	Seek additional sources of help • family members • physician (change medication) • neuropsychologist (further assessment)	• educators (teachers, aides, counselors, principal) • support professionals • parents of other children • friends • community resources (social groups)

Explained to Joshua, "Part of your protection at school is not having to go to detention. The other kids don't have that. It will make them feel bad if they know. If you tell them it will look like you're bragging. Bragging is when you think you're better than someone else."

Additional comments

Because Joshua looks so typical, his fellow students would see no reason for him to be exempt from detention. Joshua, however, had no ability (theory of mind) to think about how his reply would affect his fellow students. He could not know that his exemption would be seen as special treatment. He simply answered the question honestly. This was also the explanation that needed to be shared with the teacher, as he appeared to view the situation in the same way as the students.

Joshua's IEP was written to include this provision because the mere possibility of detention caused his anxiety level to escalate to the point where he was unable to function. In place of detention, a problem-solving process was put in place, so that any incidents could be discussed at home, allowing Joshua and his mother to problem-solve the situation and determine, discuss, and role-play what Joshua could do instead.

Thinking about others thinking—STAT Example 7.2

Step 1: Assess the situation
Kids were coming home from school. Joshua comes in first, sits down by the door to pet the dog. As Michael comes in the door, he opens it on top of Joshua's foot hurting him. Surprised to find him there, Michael, in a remorseful tone, says, "Oh, I'm sorry. I didn't know you were there." Joshua immediately turns and punches Michael in the stomach.

Step 2: Develop a hypothesis

Why? Why did they react the way they did? What could they be thinking? Select one or more of the elements below.

• Abstract language	• Motor	• Sensory	• Spatial orientation
• Control/ consistency	• Thinking about others thinking	• Social communication	• Emotions
• Mental flexibility	• Impulsive	• Executive function	• Anxiety

Hypothesis about their thinking (take a guess)

"*He hurt me. I'm going to hurt him.*" Joshua's impulsive reaction was to retaliate.

Step 3 (optional): Ask questions to obtain a step-by-step account

Types of questions

I asked, "What did you do that for?" He answered, "**He hurt me.**" I said, "He didn't do it on purpose. He said he was sorry." He insisted, "**He did do it on purpose!**" "What did Michael do to make you think he did it on purpose?" Joshua had no response.

 Revise hypothesis. Go back to Step 2

Step 2: Develop a hypothesis

Why? Why did they react the way they did? What could they be thinking? Select one or more of the elements below.

• Abstract language	• Motor	• Sensory	• Spatial orientation
• Control/ consistency	• Thinking about others thinking	• Social communication	• Emotions
• Mental flexibility	• Impulsive	• Executive function	• Anxiety

Hypothesis about their thinking (take a guess)

"*He hurt me. I'm going to hurt him.*" Joshua was not able to determine that Michael had no idea he would be on the other side of the door when he opened it. Because Joshua could not think about Michael's thinking, realizing it must have been an accident, he immediately assumed that because he was hurt Michael must have wanted to do it. Joshua's quick reaction of retaliation was a result of his impulsivity.

Step 4: Actions to consider		
Take action Take no action Explain Explain and take action	**Seek additional sources of help** • family members • physician (change medication) • neuropsychologist (further assessment)	• educators (teachers, aides, counselors, principal) • support professionals • parents of other children • friends • community resources (social groups)

I explained to Joshua, "Because Michael said, 'Oh, I'm sorry' (repeating it in the same manner), sounded like he meant it, and his face looked sad, it must have been an accident. I know you were hurt. I know it made you angry. That's OK to feel like that, but it is not OK to hit him."

Additional comments

Initially, I thought Joshua's reaction was a result of impulsivity, but after asking him questions, I revised my hypothesis. Because Joshua was not able to respond to the question about Michael's intent, I decided that his theory of mind deficit was responsible for his actions. Trying to determine the reason behind an action can oftentimes give parents or caregivers insight into what the focus for intervention should be. If I had gone with my first hypothesis of impulsivity alone, intervention would then have focused on decreasing impulsivity, missing the true root of the problem. Understanding that theory of mind played a major role in Joshua's reaction allowed me to consider Joshua's overall development and needs in that area. In addition it allowed me to provide Michael with the reason this occurred. Joshua's brothers are often confused by Joshua's reactions. An explanation of this nature helps them to better understand that Joshua's actions are not personal, but a result of not having developed in a certain area.

Chapter 8

Social Communication

"All the kids at school act like I'm invisible"—Joshua.

**"It's not my job to make sure your kid has friends"
—School administrator.**

Throughout Joshua's life people would always comment on how "smart" he was, and I would always think to myself I'd be happy to trade some of those academic skills for just a little social intelligence. God has seen fit to bless me with two children on opposite ends of the social continuum. Danny has exceptional social skills. He is easily able to size up any situation and make it work to his advantage. Danny is a master at making and keeping friends because of his ability to effectively assess a situation and act accordingly to achieve his goal. As I observe Danny in social situations, I feel confident he possesses all the skills necessary to succeed in life. While social skills don't guarantee a happy life, they certainly appear to make the journey easier. The development of social skills is, as it should be, a major concern for all parents, because social skills are necessary to build relationships throughout life. With these skills children are able to develop friendships, date, and foster business and family relationships. For Joshua, anything that involves people is hard, and everything involves people.

Social communication is complicated and complex. There is no one right way to communicate. Each of us uses social communication skills with varying degrees of expertise. Social communication involves the ability to know what to say, who to say it to, when to say it, where to say it, and how, often referred to as pragmatics. As human beings communicate with one another throughout the course of a day, these decisions are made instantaneously, many times without much thought. However, without consciously thinking about it, you have adjusted your communication to consider the other person's perspective, which is based on their sex, age, status, and personality, to name a few. Few of us stop to think about how much goes into a communicative exchange. Think about the simple act of greeting someone as you pass. The decisions you make entail who to greet versus who not to. Are they a stranger, an acquaintance, a friend, an authority figure, etc. What to say—hi, hello, what's up, hey, how are you, or nothing. When to say it—before them, after them, not at all. Where to say it: in the hallway, library, church service, baseball game, funeral, etc. How to say it: volume, tone, timing, eye contact, facial expression, body posture, body contact (hugs, high fives), personal space, etc. With all this in mind, think about how difficult it is to teach someone with social skill deficits to greet others appropriately. First, it is necessary to develop the skill. Simple as it may sound, many children have to be taught what neurotypicals naturally develop on their own. I remember telling Joshua that he needed to say hello when others said it to him. It then required further explanation as to why it was necessary. The next step involves teaching them the nuances of how to appropriately select a greeting according to the person, time, and place; all of this just to acknowledge another in what is a superficial exchange. There was Grace entering the building, ready to start the day, when she encountered a teacher who was unfamiliar with her. Grace nonchalantly greeted her with a "Hey girlie." The expression on the teacher's face was a mixture of anger and disbelief at the audacity of this student, which went unnoticed by Grace. Because a family member used this greeting in a fun way to greet Grace on a regular basis, she considered it to be a friendly way to acknowledge another, but was totally misinterpreted as disrespectful. If you can manage to get yourself in trouble with hello, then it's downhill from there when you try to engage in conversation.

When you stop to think about what's involved in a conversation, the enormity of a typical exchange becomes mind-boggling. The thought of trying to teach all they need to learn is justifiably viewed as a daunting task. Teaching the ability to initiate, maintain, and end a conversation is unquestionably difficult, yet it is only the beginning. You also must take into account what topics are an appropriate match to your partner and be able to monitor their understanding, adjusting your communication as you go. Teaching the skills is one thing, but being able to transfer them to real-world situations is never-ending, because each communicative encounter is novel and unique. It's virtually impossible to have the same conversation twice, which makes it even more difficult for rule-driven children to function. Effective social communication is not predictable. You can't simply teach a rule that will apply across the board. Nothing about conversation is formulaic.

The ability to think about others thinking changes the dynamics of conversational exchanges as they unfold. The relationship between theory of mind skills and social communication skills can be likened to the proverbial chicken and egg. Which comes first doesn't matter because they co-exist, both holding the key to successful relationships. They are interdependent, allowing us to compromise and negotiate as we exchange our thoughts, feelings, and beliefs. As people communicate, they actively monitor what others might be thinking, and adjust their social communication as they deem appropriate. Joshua's grandpa reported a conversation that took place between Joshua and his friend, Mason.

They were in the car on their way to play golf when Joshua excitedly began to talk about the latest craze among young kids, a stuffed animal that you take care of via the computer. This was the hot topic of conversation at our house among my three boys as well as the neighbor girls, but evidently for other twelve-year-old boys it wasn't the "cool" subject to pursue. Oblivious to the social cues that Mason must have been giving, Joshua continued to describe in detail his newest addition, Bucky the rabbit. Even with Mason's comment about his younger brother of three years liking them, Joshua didn't catch on. Adding to his confusion was the fact that while this was an appropriate topic for girls Joshua's age, it definitely wasn't for the boys his age. His lack of theory of mind coupled with his social skills deficit prevented him from seeing the need to adjust the flow of conversation, making for a temporarily uncomfortable environment for everyone in the car but him. As my dad recounted the story, you could almost feel him cringe.

As we refer to social communication throughout this chapter, we are defining it as any communicative exchange between two or more people that takes place in any situation, such as school, home, work, or community. Our purpose here in discussing social communication is to highlight the impact of the deficit on children with neurological differences, because it is a defining characteristic. They are unable to read the social cues of others, and also lack the ability to use social skills to communicate their intent. They can't take in the information that points to the appropriate action, even if they have the ability in social skills (but they usually don't). Deficits in the area of social communication is a problem area that compounds itself, much like an uncontrollable snowball rolling faster and faster downhill.

When you realize your child's lack of social communication skills is making it increasingly difficult to build and maintain friendships, the thought of changing schools occasionally comes to mind. When social issues reared their ugly head, it seemed like a quick fix and a good opportunity to give Joshua a clean slate, until I realized that a new school would only offer a temporary solution. It wouldn't be long before we were back to the same place we had started. The same social miscues that caused him to unwillingly alienate his peers were still present. The fact was, he didn't know what he was doing wrong or how to fix it. Once I realized a new school wasn't an option, my next thought was, we would just hold off on changing schools until his social communication problems were "fixed." Although this mindset might seem naive, it's every parent's role to problem-solve in a hopeful way, whether or not it's realistic at the moment.

Children with social deficits are often excited at the prospect of a new student entering their classroom. They see the opportunity to form a friendship with someone who has no preconceived notions of them and is willing to give them a chance because they need a friend too. A new student named Sara arrived in Joshua's class and he seized the chance to make a friend. As their friendship began to unfold, she told Joshua, "Other kids lie about you." He came home and told me, because he didn't understand what that meant. As it turned out, other children were sabotaging any chance Joshua had for friendship before it began. Clearly they shared their opinions of Joshua to Sara before she was able to make her own. Because Joshua appears to be so normal and it hasn't been publicized that he has a specific disorder, some children see him as a smart, socially inept geek, who isn't deserving of a place in the in-crowd. Fortunately, though, a few think he is fine.

Making new friends is difficult for many children. Children with neurological differences often crave the friendships and social relationships that are so far out of their reach. Unfortunately, their desire to make friends is not necessarily proportionate to their success. Grace's attempt to make new friends was like watching a disaster…a tornado working through the room, eliminating a potential friend at every stop. When one child would do something that caused everyone to laugh, she would laugh and comment, "You're weird." The children would look at her, wondering why she would say such a thing. What she meant, though, was "You're funny." She was always trying desperately to connect, so it wasn't long before she would find herself in another social predicament. One afternoon at lunch she struck up a conversation with two brothers, one of whom had a speech disorder. Grace innocently began to ask him why he spoke with an English accent. He looked at her with a puzzled look, began to squirm, and said he didn't. Instead of dropping the topic she continued on, asking the other brother why he didn't have an accent. He adamantly replied that neither one of them had an accent, and huffed away. Now Grace was the one with the puzzled look on her face, wondering once again why she found herself alone.

The impact of social communication skill deficits on one's ability to make friends became sorely apparent to me one afternoon when I had the opportunity to observe Joshua interact with an entirely new group of children. He was visiting with me at the school where I was an aide, and the atmosphere was filled with excitement because there was a "new kid in town." In the span of thirty minutes, I felt like I was watching a bad rerun as I witnessed a potential friendship die every ten minutes. Here's a description of what I saw.

Joshua, initiating a conversation about monster trucks with a boy his age said, "I have eighty-one toy monster trucks." The boy replied, "I only have three or five." Joshua said in a bragging tone, "It's going to take a long time to catch up with me." Amazingly, the conversation continued, as the boy said, "I have a Gravedigger." To which Joshua replied, "Yeah, I have three," going on to describe each one in great detail. I was sure it was over then, but this kid had endurance. Trying a different route, he continued on with, "I have a video game about monster trucks." As my stomach turned, I heard Joshua reply with, "I have two," taking several minutes to describe them in great detail. The boy asks, "Can you drive a tank in yours?" Joshua proudly boasts, "I have unlocked every course there is." The boy finally decides he's had enough and walks away. One down.

Scene two begins with Joshua wanting to play tetherball as a girl approaches, looking as if she wants to play. When Joshua didn't make any attempt to initiate a conversation, I intervened and asked the girl if she wanted to play with Joshua. She replied that she wasn't very good at tetherball. Then Joshua, true to form, responded, "I am." They then proceeded to play and Joshua very forcefully and quickly beat her. She then walked away. I was devastated, but there was still hope, as there was a line of children who wanted to play. In total, four kids came up, and four left not happy with the outcome. Joshua's play partners were not necessarily unhappy they had lost, but were reacting to the manner in which he beat them, including comments such as, "I told you I was good at this." The casualty total was now at five—six if you count me.

Oblivious to those who had come before, the next victim arrives and attempts to connect. The boy tries out several topics, but there is no response from Joshua. Out of the blue, Joshua asks the boy, "Wouldn't it be cool if you could use this tetherball as a slingshot?" The boy answers that he had made a slingshot once and it had actually turned out to be more like a catapult. Joshua looked at him, didn't acknowledge his comments, and continued with his sling-shot theme. Seven down and I can't take any more. After the boy walked away, I told Joshua that I could tell that boy wanted to be his friend. He innocently said, "He did?" Joshua really seemed to have no understanding of what had taken place.

That day I went home with a new understanding, and feeling overwhelmed with how much work still needed to be done to improve Joshua's social skills. It's one thing to know it, but to witness it gives you an entirely new perspective. That day, the importance of social skills and the impact they do and will have on his life was highlighted for me, leaving a lasting impression.

Children with neurological differences are unable effectively to respond to the social cues of others because they have difficulty reading them. As we all know, effective social communication is largely based on being able to read the social cues of your communication partner. Even if you possess the skills to respond appropriately, you can't use them unless you correctly read your partner. In sixth grade, Joshua would repeatedly greet his friend, Mason, in the school hallway by putting his arm around him almost in a side-by-side hug. Mason, who is extremely socially savvy, was bothered by how this greeting might be perceived by their peers. He initially tried to use nonverbal signals to communicate his discomfort. When that didn't work, he verbally requested that Joshua stop. Even then, Joshua continued with this form of greeting. In all prob-ability, he did this because school hallways provide an unpredictable and stress-ful setting. Over the years, Mason has always proved to be a kind, safe person who has helped facilitate positive social interaction, so Joshua often seeks him out. He would never intentionally do anything to alienate Mason. Once Mason showed him what to do instead, which was to replace the hug with a new hand-shake, the situation was resolved. It makes me feel sad to wonder how many potential friendships were sacrificed by Joshua's inability to read social cues. Teaching him what to do instead is always a great first step.

Children diagnosed with neurological differences are often unable to relate an event as it happened because they don't have the communication skills of explanation. The information they provide may be too much or not enough, and they also lack the ability to monitor the understanding of their communica-tion partner. Although not always totally accurate, there usually is enough of the truth present to make the story sound possible, although not probable. As a parent you hear their story, which has typically caused them to become upset, and your initial reaction is a defensive one. In this case, Joshua caused the situation to be misinterpreted. He called home in tears in sixth grade. He told me his aide had "ripped his research paper into pieces and threw it in the garbage." As you can imagine, my visceral response was not a good one, but I decided to take a deep breath and check out the facts. I had to keep telling myself that I only had his version and his version was not always completely accurate. However, I knew this was what he believed to be true and was reacting to.

After hours of phone calls with school personnel, I found out what really occurred. As it turned out, the classroom aide had written numerous corrections on Joshua's paper, explaining that he needed to redo a large part. When she was confronted with the allegation that she had ripped up his paper, she was surprised, denying it vehemently. Hearing her denial, Joshua, using a mildly irritated tone, enlightened her to the fact that when he used "ripping a paper to shreds" it was simply a figure of speech. Parents' problem-solve situations with their children, based on the information they receive from them. In this case, because Joshua wasn't able to explain the situation accurately, my initial reaction was one of anger as I contemplated confronting the aide. Waiting and collecting additional information allowed me to get the whole picture, resulting in a completely different course of action. I have learned over the years the importance of listening and believing—but also investigating further.

It is important to consider the role a lack of social skills might play when attempting to assess a child's behavior. In third grade, on some occasions, Grace would make her entrance into her classroom by surprising her unsuspecting classmate with a smack to the back of their head. Obviously, her peer was angry, she was oblivious, and the chance of developing a friendship was greatly diminished. At first glance, her actions could be considered mean-spirited, but if you asked her if she intended to be mean to that student, she would have responded with a resounding no, shocked at the possibility. The question then became, why, what was she trying to accomplish? The classroom aide thought that her actions were really an attempt to greet her "friend." By analyzing the situation from a social communication perspective, the course of action to be taken changes from one of punishment to telling and showing her what to do instead.

As every parent of a child with a neurological difference of this type can attest, his or her child is often viewed as rude and disrespectful. This becomes a major problem in the school setting because these children don't have the social communication ability to talk to people according to their position in the world. Therefore, they see themselves as being of equal status with teachers, principals, and other adults. They approach everyone the same way, using the same vocabulary, tone of voice, and body language, lacking what is referred to in the speech and language world as the ability to change registers. They have only one way to communicate with everyone. What they got is what you get. So often Grace's attempts to connect with adults were viewed negatively, as she asked incessant streams of personal questions, such as, "Who called you? What did they want? Where are you going? Who's going with you?" These are questions that everyone has but knows not to ask. However, when a child asks these questions of an adult they can be viewed as manipulative and inappropriate. Requests are presented as if they are commands, such as, "Well, aren't you going to heat up my lunch?" when what was really meant was, "Will you please heat up my lunch?" Simple classroom tasks can quickly lead to punishment, as on the occasion when Joshua, in fourth grade, was the last one in the class to take his book up to the teacher to be bound and said, "Well finally," with a huff. His intent was not disrespectful; it was simply a response to a long wait. The result was yet another lost recess.

In elementary school, withholding recess seems to be the discipline measure of choice, so often the social communication deficit results in a loss of recess, which in reality is probably the most important part of the child's day. Recess is one of the few consistent opportunities children have to engage in unstructured social communication during the school day, so it is sad that they often miss it. Knowing how important reading and math are for the child's success, no teacher would ever think to say, "You can't participate today because you were disrespectful." Unfortunately, schools so often think their job is only to focus on academic curriculum, but we all know that so much of life's successes are dependent on social communication abilities. Neurotypical children naturally use recess to develop their social communication skills. Recess is a learning opportunity that is often wasted when, in fact, it is time that should be used as an extension of the classroom—especially for children with social communication disorders. How often I thought this when Joshua would come home and tell me that at indoor recess his time was spent at his desk, alone, doing homework. Leaving a child with social deficits at recess without support is like throwing a child who can't swim into a pool without a life jacket. It would take very little to turn this nightmare called recess into an enjoyable social experience that would allow them to develop skills that will benefit them throughout life. Adults or peers could easily be used to facilitate the naturally occurring conversations and interactions by ensuring their success. Successful interactions lead to friendships. Forever etched in my memory are the many days I spent watching from a distance, as Joshua walked the perimeter of the playground by himself with his head down, not engaged with anyone, in what seemed to be a sad metaphor for his life. I sure wasn't sad to see recess go in sixth grade, and now all we had to worry about was getting through lunch.

Lunch became a bigger problem when we hit junior high. Now lunchtime became longer, and staggered schedules determined whom you could choose to sit with. This lunchroom dynamic requires students to develop an entirely new set of social skills, many of which are unspoken. For me more than for Joshua, this created great anxiety. I knew he was unable to navigate this social scene and would often come home reporting that he sat alone. The thought of this broke my heart. It was like watching him walking around that playground alone, all over again. What had the potential to have a huge, negative social effect was averted with minimal effort by school personnel. Joshua and I created a list of possible lunch partners, which we passed along to the support educator so she could determine if they would like to sit with him. From there we developed a schedule, so that Joshua knew who he was sitting with on which days, and they knew to expect him, so there was always a seat available. A little attention at the beginning of the year took Joshua from a place of isolation to an opportunity to foster friendships.

It is necessary for parents and educators to facilitate the formation of social groups wherever possible, because these children are unable to become members of social groups on their own. Without assistance, they often end up isolated and socially vulnerable, becoming easy prey for bullies. Bullying is accomplished in a variety of ways. There's the more direct approach. In fifth grade, Joshua was abnormally anxious about leaving for school one morning. He fell to the floor, crying and saying he just couldn't go. After much discussion and probing, I figured out there were two boys who had been calling him names, like "geek" and "nerd" every time he passed them. He could conceivably have passed them hundreds of times a day, and I could never determine how long this had been going on. The abuse must have been relentless for Joshua to refuse to go to school, because to him going to school is a rule, and he always follows the rules. The damage to his self-esteem was one obvious result, but what makes a situation like this seem overwhelming is his inability to address it. He doesn't know what to say, how to act, or know how, or where to obtain help. Bad as it was, this situation concerned Joshua's relationship only with these two boys.

Other types of bullying can have more far-reaching effects. For example, in sixth grade, everything seemed to be going well. Things at school seemed to be at a plateau, when one day, Joshua engaged in what seemed to be an innocent conversation with three girls his age on the bus. They asked him, "Do you go out with Kevin?" Joshua replied, "Yes." That night at a party, those same girls told a boy Joshua's age, who was a family friend, that Joshua was gay. They replayed the entire conversation. The boy told them that wasn't true, and Joshua just didn't understand what they meant by their question. Luckily, the boy told his mom, who apprised me of the situation. In the course of discussing his conversation with the girls, he was shocked to learn that "going out with someone," meant dating them. Because he and Kevin had gone places together, he innocently answered their question, never having any idea of the potential consequences. From Joshua's perspective, this event never registered as having any importance. However, this single exchange, if never corrected, could have impacted the willingness of his peers to entertain the possibility of a friendship.

The presence of a social communication deficit can cause a child to be the constant target of bullies. The previous examples illustrate two different types of bullying. Because of his social communication deficit, Joshua really only viewed the first example as bullying, and never gave the second any thought, although it could have been the most damaging. Inability to read, understand, and react to social cues, coupled with their naïveté resulting from their mindblindness, makes these children potential victims for bullies, as well as predators. Those who love them need to be ever mindful of their vulnerability and make it their job to protect them.

Children with neurological differences are typically unable to view social situations as other children do. They haven't developed an understanding that people often say things they don't mean, and mean things they don't say, so they often misinterpret situations that arise. Their interpretation of the situation, correct or not, is the perception that drives their actions and reactions. As a result, they have difficulty developing friendships, which leads to a limited or non-existent social network. Because their social network is limited, they are left with few people to discuss how to navigate the problems of life. The effects of the deficit are cumulative, resulting in limited or non-existent friendships, and have the potential to cause social isolation. Most people only find a few "real friends" in life if they are lucky. These special friendships develop out of a lifetime of social encounters with many people who start out as acquaintances. These children's ability to develop solid lasting relationships is limited, first by the number of successful encounters they have with acquaintances, then by their ability to nurture the relationship through meaningful conversations and shared experiences.

In summary, social communication is about reading situations and adapting in what is always a constant state of change. It is critical that social communication be a major focus of intervention. It should include providing the child with successful social encounters, with detailed explanations about what they do right and what they need to change, and what to do instead. As parents dream about the lives of their children, they all want the final outcome to be one of happiness. In the typical scenario, that would include a job that allows them to have a roof over their head, food to eat, and someone to share it with. The key to acquiring these is social skills. When you have a child with a neurological difference, these dreams are the same, but the life planning requires a greater effort and must take social skills into account. I often think that I could be at peace if I could be assured that Joshua could find that one person to share his life with, who could love him for who he is.

Things to consider

- Tell the child when they do something correctly, and explain why it was correct.

- If they don't know how to perform a social skill, teach them what to do, when to do it, what to say, how your face and body look when you do it, and explain why you do it.

- Focus on improving only one or two social skills at a time. Select those skills that make the child "stick out" and skills that can be used in a variety of settings and will have the biggest positive impact on their life.

- In place of an inappropriate social skill, teach them what they should do instead.

- Rehearse social situations.

- Watch TV, movies, people in public, and talk about what the characters are doing and why. Explain the social skills observed.

- At times when the child seems rude or uncaring, ask if they intended to hurt the other person's feelings.

- Progress can be slow, so don't give up, keep explaining.

- Place the child in social situations where they can feel success, facilitating where possible. Look for groups of children with similar interests.

- Communicating via the computer can often facilitate success because the child only needs to focus on the message in print, without the need to read social cues.

- Decide whether or not to tell other kids about the child's social needs and how to react to them.

Social communication—STAT Example 8.1

Step 1: Assess the situation
After having been at school only 15 minutes one morning, Joshua called home crying uncontrollably. He said he had done something awful and was sorry. When I asked him what he had done, he said, "I called someone a really bad name. My teacher said it's inappropriate to call someone something other than their name."

Step 2: Develop a hypothesis

Why? Why did they react the way they did? What could they be thinking? Select one or more of the elements below.

• Abstract language	• Motor	• Sensory	• Spatial orientation
• Control/ consistency	• Thinking about others thinking	• Social communication	• Emotions
• Mental flexibility	• Impulsive	• Executive function	• Anxiety

Hypothesis about their thinking (take a guess)

"You did or said something mean to me and I'm saying something mean back."

Step 3 (optional): Ask questions to obtain a step-by-step account

Types of questions

"What name did you call the boy?" **"Percival."** "Who's Percival and why did you call him that?" **"It's the name of a character in an animated movie. I was just trying to be funny."** "Let me talk to your teacher." The teacher said "the boy came to me and said that Joshua had called him a pussy."

Revise hypothesis. Go back to Step 2

Step 2: Develop a hypothesis

Why? Why did they react the way they did? What could they be thinking? Select one or more of the elements below.

• Abstract language	• Motor	• Sensory	• Spatial orientation
• Control/ consistency	• Thinking about others thinking	• Social communication	• Emotions
• Mental flexibility	• Impulsive	• Executive function	• Anxiety

Hypothesis about their thinking (take a guess)

After talking to the teacher and Joshua, I realized Joshua was misinterpreted. He never intended to call anyone a bad name. In his mind he was saying, *"I was trying to be funny. I am calling you Percival and I thought you would find it funny too."*

Step 4: Actions to consider

Take action	**Seek additional sources of help**	• educators (teachers, aides, counselors, principal)
Take no action	• family members	• support professionals
	• physician (change medication)	• parents of other children
Explain		• friends
	• neuropsychologist (further assessment)	• community resources (social groups)
Explain and take action		

I explained to the teacher that we do not use that type of language in our home. Joshua was using a name of a character from a movie and was trying to be funny. He didn't understand that he had done anything wrong because in his mind he used the name Percival. I later talked to Joshua and explained that he had been misunderstood and that the boy and teacher thought he had used a nasty name, but that the teacher now knew he had not.

Additional comments

Originally, I thought the boy had done something mean to Joshua, and that he had acted impulsively in calling him a bad name. I knew I needed more information when Joshua told me the name he had called him was Percival, because I couldn't understand why this had caused such an upset. After questioning the teacher, I realized there was a discrepancy in the two stories. When the teacher told me what name he had used, I assured her we did not use that kind of language in our home and was sure Joshua didn't even know what that term meant.

This situation escalated into a problem because Joshua was unable to read the situation. He didn't realize what had gone wrong and did not have the social communication skills to explain his thinking to the boy or the teacher. It was only through targeted questioning that his thinking was made clear to all parties.

Every time I think back to that morning, I remember how amazed I was that it took only fifteen minutes in school before Joshua was in a situation that warranted a phone call home.

Even though the situation was resolved, the damage to Joshua had already been done. Once again he had found himself in a situation where he was being blamed for something he didn't do.

Social communication—STAT Example 8.2

Step 1: Assess the situation
In the fifth grade, Joshua had a top-notch special educator who was instrumental in making a positive change in his school life. One afternoon in she called home to inform me that they had lost Joshua during field day. They searched and found him in another classroom. They talked with Joshua and he said that he had motioned with his thumb to the teacher that he was going to the other classroom. The teacher said the problem was that he never got her attention.

Step 2: Develop a hypothesis

Why? Why did they react the way they did? What could they be thinking? Select one or more of the elements below.

• Abstract language	• Motor	• Sensory	• Spatial orientation
• Control/ consistency	• Thinking about others thinking	• Social communication	• Emotions
• Mental flexibility	• Impulsive	• Executive function	• Anxiety

Hypothesis about their thinking (take a guess)

"I told them where I was. I am where I indicated I would be."

Step 3 (optional): Ask questions to obtain a step-by-step account

Types of questions

"What happened?" Joshua said he gave the teacher a sign to let her know he was going in. "Was the teacher looking at you when you gave her the sign?" Joshua said, **"No, she had her back to me talking with three other kids."**

 Revise hypothesis. Go back to Step 2

Step 4: Actions to consider

Take action	**Seek additional sources of help**	• educators (teachers, aides, counselors, principal)
Take no action	• family members	• support professionals
	• physician (change medication)	• parents of other children
Explain		• friends
	• neuropsychologist (further assessment)	• community resources (social groups)
Explain and take action		

I explained to Joshua when you signal someone you need to make sure you get a response from them such as a head nod, thumbs up, or wave so you know they got the message.

Additional comments

When I talked with Joshua, he was quite surprised at the teacher's concern because in his mind he had communicated where he would be. He didn't have the social communication skills to know that he needed to receive acknowledgement of his message. On the bright side, his use of a nonverbal communication signal (a pointing thumb) showed development in communicating in this way. If he had not been identified as having a neurological deficit, it would be hard for educators to believe this wasn't intentional negative behavior.

Chapter 9

Emotions

**"I feel like I'm going to cry but I don't know why"
—Grace.**

It's hard to believe that a child eleven years old could look directly at someone who has tears streaming down their cheeks, and appear not to be affected in any way. One afternoon, Joshua came into my room unexpectedly when I was crying. Looking directly at me and without hesitation, he asked where his monster truck was. I responded and he went on his way while I sat shell-shocked by what had just transpired. Initially, I was scrambling for an explanation for him, but before I knew it, the event was over and I didn't need one. Talk about a mix of emotions as I quickly went from anxiety to relief, to disbelief, shock, and confusion. I couldn't believe what I had just seen and what I felt about it. It was chilling. This was a defining moment. There was no denying there was a big problem.

As we all know, emotions are complicated and complex because there are so many, each having its own varying degrees of intensity. Oftentimes Joshua misses the signals of mild annoyance, oblivious of their presence until he's faced with all-out fury, which he meets with great shock and surprise. Emotions are instinctive to most of us and don't require any explanation. We easily read the social cues of others and ascribe an emotion to them, which in turn drives our interactions with that person. Emotions are directly intertwined with theory of mind and social communication skills. Think about meeting a friend for lunch. You walk into the restaurant and there you see your friend sitting in a booth with their head down, slumped shoulders, and looking up at you with a somber face. Instinctively, your first reaction is to ask what is wrong. However, if you walked in and were met with a smile and a wave, you would proceed with a warm greeting accompanied by a lighthearted comment. So much has been conveyed, yet nothing has been said. As we go through our day, we are always assessing the emotions of those with whom we interact. Because it's an innate ability for most of us in varying degrees, it makes it extremely difficult to understand how the absence of this ability affects the lives of those diagnosed with neurological differences.

While attending a wedding recently, I observed Grace, who was a member of the wedding party, stiffly and uncomfortably walk around the reception alone, making several laps around the room. Up to this point, all the wedding activities had been pretty much scripted and gone according to plan. A few people who knew of her diagnosis engaged Grace in conversation; however, others in the crowd steered clear. As you talk to Grace, her speech is very monotone and robotic, seemingly void of any feeling or emotion. However, anyone who really knew Grace would know there was nothing further from the truth. She desperately wanted to connect, but didn't know how to make it happen. It's moments like these that highlight the important role emotions play in every aspect of our life. One of the biggest misconceptions about children diagnosed with a neurological deficit is that they have no feelings. It's easy to see how one could come to that conclusion, but they are filled with the same emotions every other human being has, only lacking the ability to identify and know what to do with them.

Feelings provoke a physical response, which we then identify consciously or unconsciously, and act upon. Diagnosed children have the physical response, but because they can't identify it, and don't know what to do with it, this often-times leads to anxiety, upset, or meltdowns. As they develop, they are able, at times, to identify the four basic emotions most easily depicted as *happy, sad, mad,* and *afraid,* but the gradients of each continue to elude them. The more abstract the emotions, such as embarrassed, proud, guilty, hopeful, determined, curious, confident, compassionate, insecure, relaxed, and nervous, the more difficult they are for them to grasp. In kindergarten, Joshua spent many speech therapy sessions looking at a book of faces that depicted the four basic emotions, which he was asked to identify over and over and over again. His speech therapist assured me he had a strong grasp of these emotions, never really understanding that to him the exercise was the equivalent of a rote task, such as flashcards.

Unfortunately, when real-life situations arose where identifying one of those emotions would have helped him, he was unable to do so.

It was a rude awakening for me to realize that Joshua would need an explanation for how to feel. I remember having to explain to him, in detail, the appropriate response to someone falling down and getting hurt. I explained that he needed to go to them and ask if they were all right. I later saw him do just that at the appropriate time. My sense of accomplishment was outweighed by the overwhelming understanding that he potentially required an explanation about every situation he would encounter. For him it began as simply procedural, but as he developed I was able to witness some presence of emotion behind the act.

By fourth grade, a focus of Joshua's speech therapy home plan was to help identify his emotions for him during everyday situations. For example, if I knew Joshua was excited about an imminent event, I would talk through with him how he physically felt, and then label the feeling for him. Another tool that proved to be beneficial was using a 0–10 scale to help him communicate the intensity of his emotions, so that I could help him to interpret what he was feeling and put it in perspective. It would help us to identify how nervous or anxious he was about a situation, and help to determine how to problem-solve it. It still is an effective tool that can be used anywhere by anyone. Joshua was eventually able to identify physical changes by telling me he had a funny feeling in his stomach. From there, we would talk and try to identify what he felt and why. This was such a relief, because prior to this Joshua's emotions would go unidentified, building to the point of great anxiety and causing physical illness.

Just when you think you have one problem solved, another one appears. When you are forced to explain what seems to be everything in great detail, you start to realize how much you take for granted and how complicated emotions really are. I found out just how confusing emotions can be as I tried to explain to Joshua how people could have two feelings about one event. For example, I remember Joshua telling me that he was happy that school was out for the year, but asking why he felt sad. I had never until then thought about the idea that one event could elicit two emotions. Similarly, when I was talking to Danny one day, it led me to think further about one event causing two people to feel differently. It still brings a smile to my face to think about Danny coming to me, appalled and disgusted at the idea that the mothers in the neighborhood were having a party the first day of school. He just couldn't imagine that being without their children would be a cause for mothers to celebrate. I began to think about how difficult it would be for Joshua to grasp this idea about emotions, because of his lack of theory of mind. As I continue to explain ongoing emotional events to Joshua, I realize how illogical emotions are. While watching a funny movie, I was laughing so hard I had tears streaming down my face. Joshua asked, "Why are you crying?" I explained, "Because it's so funny." He replied, "If it's so funny, why are you crying?" When you have to answer a question like this, you realize how often what we do doesn't make sense. How confusing all of this must be when you attempt to think about emotions logically.

Think about their world. Children with neurological differences don't know what they are feeling, much less what to do about it. Meanwhile, other people are making judgements based on their perceptions of what they think these children are feeling. The lack of development in the areas of theory of mind and social skills, coupled with emotions, frequently can cause a continuous cycle of dysfunction. Even at age twelve, problems like this frequently continue to arise with Joshua. I can't recall the exact source of this particular problem, but Danny was quite frustrated with something Joshua had done and decided that talking wasn't working. Danny decided he would write his concerns down and present them to Joshua in an attempt to get a response from Joshua to resolve the issue. Danny, confident in his fail-safe plan, presented his written piece to Joshua. Joshua took the pen from Danny and promptly corrected the grammar and spelling mistakes, returning it to Danny with a superior attitude. In his frustration, Danny decided to scrap the plan and resorted to Plan A—screaming, which was once again met with a puzzled look from Joshua. If I didn't live it, I wouldn't believe it. Having to deal with this type of response on a frequent basis often leaves Danny questioning Joshua's love for him. Although I can't explain Joshua's reaction, I believe he does love Danny, but his limited skills leave a different message. Joshua's actions and reactions make it that much more difficult to convince Danny of this. As a parent, trying to repair that kind of damage on a regular basis is emotionally exhausting.

The way others perceive the emotions of these children is often far from the way it really is. Basing reactions solely on what you see is definitely a mistake. What you see is very rarely what you get. The summer Joshua was ten years old, Todd, Joshua's dad, fell and hurt himself while building a deck. Because he needed medical attention, I was trying to quickly load the boys in the van. Because of my panicked reaction, family chaos ensued. Danny and Michael quickly picked up on my emotions and were in a state of immediate distress. Joshua, on the other hand, appeared quite calm, stating that he would be back momentarily as he went off to retrieve something. He returned holding his favorite teddy bear, which, I immediately assumed, would be comforting to him as we went through this trauma. As Todd lay there in excruciating pain, Joshua gently placed the bear next to his face. Previous to this action, I would have thought that Joshua was not impacted in any way, because outwardly he looked to be unfazed.

As we move through our world, we continually make assessments of people and the type of relationship, if any, we want to pursue. Relationships develop based on two people receiving mutually beneficial emotional support. Emotional reciprocity is a necessary component of forming relationships. Emotions are conveyed through social skills, so without those skills your ability to form emotional relationships that are mutually beneficial is greatly diminished. To be effective, individuals need to be able to identify their own emotions, understand them, and know how to convey them in order to get a desired response. However, once accomplished, this same process must occur when dealing with others in order to have successful relationships. It's big. Children with neurological disorders don't know how they feel. They don't know how others feel. So, how can they begin to form a relationship?

Danny and Michael's attempts to show their brotherly affection to Joshua are often met with less than stellar results. Often Danny's nightly attempts to offer Joshua a hug are met with no response. Yet, if you ask Joshua if he loves his brothers, he responds with a matter-of-fact "Well, of course I do." Joshua's limited ability to provide emotional reciprocity obviously spills over into the area of friendships. Up until fourth grade, Joshua found the suggestion of playing with someone other than his best friend Nick totally inappropriate. He viewed it as a betrayal of their friendship. However, when asked who his friends were, Joshua would rattle off a list of children who were simply acquaintances. His definition of friendship is shaky at best. Friendship, for him, means someone who is kind to you. Even at twelve, he doesn't have an understanding of initiating, developing, and maintaining a relationship. It's only recently that he on very rare occasions thinks to invite someone over. Much of the time he prefers to be alone, but expects his friends to remain his friends without any maintenance of the relationship.

If forming friendships with boys is difficult, the topic of girlfriends takes us to a new possibility for yet more unexplainable confusion. Even neurotypicals have difficulty making sense of romantic relationships. In fourth grade Joshua developed his first crush. As I began to try to explain to Joshua the intricacies of boy–girl relationships, I realized how ridiculous I sounded. It went something like this. "Joshua, if you want her to like you, you can't act like you like her too much." "But, I do." "I know, but you can't act like that because you need to play hard to get." "Then how will she know that I like her?" After several rounds of chasing my tail, I was once again left with those words of wisdom, "Because I said so." You can't help but empathize with the plight of these children as they naturally develop and attempt to pursue meaningful romantic relationships. These unspoken, unwritten rules of romantic relationships don't make sense, making their pursuit that much more difficult.

As usual, school poses its own set of problems where emotions are concerned. It starts in kindergarten when you feel the need to preface your child's behavior by telling the teacher your child doesn't share and shows no empathy. As you continue explaining, you are desperately trying to prove that you really are a loving, caring family that has tried to teach those values. No matter what you say, there is always that unspoken insinuation that at the core of the problem is your parenting. Unfortunately, this perception continues on as your child progresses through the grades, because their emotional development is always significantly lagging when compared to their peers. As Joshua and I walked into the junior high building for his first visit, he thought nothing of holding my hand as we proceeded down the hall. I knew that because of his anxiety level, Joshua needed that emotional support, but I was also concerned about the judgmental eyes of others. Once again, because the child looks too good, it makes it impossible for the majority of people they encounter to believe the extent of their needs. When people encounter a child in a wheelchair with obvious special needs, they approach, as they should, with an attitude of openness and compassion. However, children whose neurological differences are not as readily apparent are held to a different standard, even though their needs in many areas are the same. When people believe there is a need, they approach the child from a place of patience and understanding. If these children could simply be viewed in this manner, the quality of their life would be drastically improved.

Throughout the years, when I have tried to convey to educators the depth of Joshua's difficulties in the school setting, the response is always not to worry, because he looks so happy. They proceed to tell me how they have observed him throughout the day and he is smiling. Those educators who have been kind enough, on a regular basis, to ask Joshua how he was doing, always get the same response of "I'm fine." It's the rare few that have been able to realize that his emotions don't typically match his outward demeanor or answers. Just because he smiles and says he's fine, doesn't mean he is. That's been hard for many to understand. Another example is one that occurred during his twelve-year-old check-up when the nurse commented on how rare it was to see a child so happy to be there, because Joshua was continually laughing and smiling. I had to explain to her that he wasn't happy at all, in fact, he was extremely nervous.

The inability to comprehend the social signaling of emotions can have a negative impact academically. In school, by third grade, the characters in a literary text are described in a more inferential way. Students are expected to draw conclusions about the characters' personality based on those clues. The ability to infer and to think abstractly about emotions is required throughout school, if children are to have a deeper understanding of the text. For example, the text indicates the character's face was red and the veins on his neck were popping out. Based on the information presented in the surrounding text, the child needs to infer that the character is angry, yet the text never comes out and says that. Although this is a simple example, as the students continue to advance grade levels, the inferential skills required are more complex and ubiquitous.

As students study poetry and literature, they are often asked to determine the mood the author intends to convey. Oftentimes the assignments require students to select words, phrases, and images that provide the reader with the feelings intended by the author. Not only do they have to find the feeling words; they are typically required to explain what those words convey and how they know. If the emotions the children are able to discuss are limited to the basic four, the final grade can be drastically impacted. (When presented with text rich with inferential figurative language and asked to identify the mood of the piece, Joshua's response to three different excerpts was "the mood is sort of sorry and sad," "the mood is happy," and "the mood could be sad.") As students, this puts them at a definite disadvantage, simply because they don't have the ability to understand their own feelings, much less the feelings an author is trying to convey.

Emotions are the criteria by which we judge the quality of our lives. Emotions are an integral part of every aspect of our lives, from the relationships we form to the movies we watch and the books we read. We use our emotions as the basis for determining the many decisions we make throughout our lives. Children with neurological differences feel everything everyone else does. They feel it but they don't understand it. They don't understand it, so they don't know what to do with it. They don't *know* what they feel, which makes it more difficult to make decisions and move forward in life. It must be difficult enough not to know how you feel, but then to have others react to how they *think* you feel can only add enormous stress to your life. Emotions are the lens through which people view their world. It's the job of those who love these children to help them see as close to 20/20 as they can.

Things to consider

- Don't assume you know how the child feels based solely on their outward appearance.

- As situations present themselves throughout the day, talk out loud about what you feel and why you feel that way.

- At times when you have a good idea about what the child might be feeling, identify their feelings for them and relate it to the physical feeling they may be having.

- Point out both the obvious and the subtle social cues that convey certain emotions.

- Explain their atypical responses to those who are willing to listen, especially siblings who may be feeling the negative impact.

- Teach them to use the 0–10 scale to identify the intensity of their feelings.

- While reading or watching television, discuss the characters' feelings, why they might feel that way, and the clues that make you think so.

Emotions—STAT Example 9.1

Step 1: Assess the situation

Josh, around age five, threw something at me while I was lying on the floor and accidentally hit me in the head. I grabbed my head and began to cry. Josh's younger brother, Danny, rushed over and asked "Mommy, Mommy are you okay?" Then, he ran to get a box of tissues. Josh, standing three feet away, started screaming, "Stop it! Stop it!"

Step 2: Develop a hypothesis

Why? Why did they react the way they did? What could they be thinking? Select one or more of the elements below.

• Abstract language	• Motor	• Sensory	• Spatial orientation
• Control/ consistency	• Thinking about others thinking	• Social communication	• Emotions
• Mental flexibility	• Impulsive	• Executive function	• Anxiety

Hypothesis about their thinking (take a guess)

"Everybody is upset. My mom is hurt. My mom takes care of me, if something happens to her, who will take care of me?"

↓

Step 3 (optional): Ask questions to obtain a step-by-step account

Types of questions

[Not needed in this example]

↓ ↳ Revise hypothesis. Go back to Step 2

Step 4: Actions to consider

Take action	**Seek additional sources of help**
Take no action	• family members • physician (change medication) • neuropsychologist (further assessment)
Explain	• educators (teachers, aides, counselors, principal) • support professionals • parents of other children • friends • community resources (social groups)
Explain and take action	

As I held Joshua and attempted to console him, I reassured him I would be all right and he didn't have to worry.

Additional comments

Joshua was unable to identify his own emotions, and therefore was unable to determine what he should do. His reaction could easily have been viewed as an inappropriate emotional response. A third party looking at the situation would think Joshua was an unkind, uncaring child who was choosing not to help his mother. While both children were afraid, Danny's was an appropriate response, because it was one that took my feelings into consideration and provided consolation. Even though Danny was younger, he had developed theory of mind and emotional intelligence at a level that far surpassed Joshua. This situation highlights the connection between the development of theory of mind and emotional response. In reality, Joshua didn't have the ability to identify my emotions or his own.

I did not provide any in-depth explanation about appropriate emotional reactions at that time because, first of all, Joshua was too upset to receive the information, and second, he had not developed theory of mind and emotional intelligence enough to understand.

Emotions—STAT Example 9.2

Step 1: Assess the situation

While having dinner, Joshua insisted on telling Leslie H-P about Danny singing karaoke on a family vacation. Although Danny had done well overall, Joshua felt the need to discuss the one song where Danny was unable to keep up with the words. As the discussion continued, you could see the detrimental effect on Danny's self-esteem through his facial expression, body language, and overall physical demeanor. Oblivious to Danny's emotional response, Joshua persisted in his verbal attack.

Step 2: Develop a hypothesis

Why? Why did they react the way they did? What could they be thinking? Select one or more of the elements below.

• Abstract language	• Motor	• Sensory	• Spatial orientation
• Control/ consistency	• Thinking about others thinking	• Social communication	• Emotions
• Mental flexibility	• Impulsive	• Executive function	• Anxiety

Hypothesis about their thinking (take a guess)

"Everybody is always talking about how great Danny sings and that makes me angry. I want to tell Leslie H-P about a time when he wasn't perfect. I don't care how it makes Danny feel, I want her to think I'm more talented than Danny." Joshua is jealous of Danny's singing ability and doesn't know how to identify or deal with that emotion.

Step 3 (optional): Ask questions to obtain a step-by-step account
Types of questions
[Not needed in this example]

 Revise hypothesis. Go back to Step 2

Step 4: Actions to consider

Take action	**Seek additional sources of help**	• educators (teachers, aides, counselors, principal)
Take no action	• family members	• support professionals
	• physician (change medication)	• parents of other children
Explain	• neuropsychologist (further assessment)	• friends
Explain and take action		• community resources (social groups)

Leslie H-P saw Danny's deflated demeanor across the table and told him that she had heard from his mother that he really did a great job. She continued by saying how courageous he was to get up in front of everyone and sing and what a great singer she knew he was. She then turned to telling Joshua he was courageous also when he played the trombone in front of people. She told Joshua not to tell Danny he wasn't good because that made Danny feel bad. She proceeded to tell all three boys how important it was that they encourage one another.

Additional comments

Joshua doesn't have the ability to identify his own jealousy. As a result, he has no way to manage this feeling, so his only way to deal with it is to be negative about Danny's abilities. His focus is on himself without any thought or response to Danny's reaction or feelings. Although this seems totally negative, the bright spot is that this situation shows development in his theory of mind abilities. In this scenario, he is working to diminish Danny's skills in an effort to make Leslie H-P think he has more talent.

Chapter 10

Mental Flexibility

"Why should I guess and possibly be wrong when I can figure out the exact answer and know I'm right?"
—Joshua on estimation.

In fourth grade, Joshua told me he had lost his recess at school that day, seemingly unaffected, as he had grown quite accustomed to life without recess. I asked him why and he said, "Because I answered the phone. What's wrong with answering the phone?" Thinking he might have said something inappropriate, I asked him what he said when he picked it up. He told me he said, "Hello, Mrs. K's room." I then asked what his teacher said to him. He said she used a mean voice to say, "The phone is not to be used by children." Joshua then said to me, "Mom, no one ever told me I couldn't answer the phone. How was I supposed to know?" His question made me think, how did all the other students in the room know not to answer the phone, and why didn't he? I was quite sure that it wasn't because he missed school the day they gave the phone orientation. Somehow, though, he was the only one who didn't get it. As I viewed the situation from his perspective, I could understand how answering the phone made sense. That's what people do when the phone rings, answer it. I could understand his thinking. I could even justify it. However, it was quite evident that his thinking was different from that of the other twenty-nine children in the room, who knew not to answer the phone.

Children with neurological differences often view the world in black-and-white. Unfortunately, so much of the world is gray and left to individual interpretation that they need an interpreter for many situations that arise. The world they see is one of details, facts, and parts, all arranged in a logical order. Typically, one of their greatest strengths lies in their accurate memory. They naturally use this combination and look to apply it wherever possible, as this is one of their only means of interpreting their surroundings. Anything you can explain to them in a logical way with an emphasis on steps and details gives them the best chance for success, because those are the skills they have.

The focus on facts in and of itself is not a problem, it is the inability to be mentally flexible with those facts that is the problem. "Flexible" conjures up all types of images that make you think about someone who can go with the flow and take life as it comes. A flexible thinker is someone who easily adapts and adjusts to the situation before him or her. To be a flexible thinker you have to look at a situation and understand the big picture, know that there is more than one way to do something, and know that the way you do something in one situation is not necessarily the way you do it in another. Joshua once returned from a family vacation and brought Leslie H-P an assortment of tea bags. After presenting them to her, he quickly followed with a list outlining the order in which they were to be consumed. Why he selected that order, or why the order was even important to him, is a mystery; however, he was insistent that his instructions be followed.

Focusing on detail is a characteristic that impedes the ability of children with a neurological difference to be flexible thinkers. As young children, they explore their world with a focus on detail. Often when they receive a toy they are more interested in its parts than how to use it, which can result in toys being broken as they undergo inspection. So often their focus on parts changes the outcome of an experience. When Joshua was very young our family went to an amusement park for the day. He and I were sitting in a ride which was a car that was slowly moving in a circle around the center. I expected Joshua to happily take the wheel and pretend he was driving. When I looked over ready to see a smiling race car driver, what I saw was his bottom in the air with his body hanging over the side of the car. It was clear that his enjoyment was coming from trying to determine how the car was moving, rather than pretending to drive it like all the other children around us.

As Joshua grew, the attention to detail continued, as his Christmas list always included a request for a book of world records. Each year he wanted the latest version and I knew it had better be hardbound in order to withstand the use. If I could just get him on a game show the information would pay off, but other than that the only purpose it serves is to entertain him, which is purpose enough for me. On the other hand, this attention to detail is beneficial when he is able to instantly pick out our car in a parking lot, based solely on the type of tires we have. Most of us find our cars by color and shape, while he chooses tires. What seems unimportant to most of us can be important to the child. Grace's family was talking about a new car they had just purchased. Never having seen the car, you would expect her first question to revolve around the color and make. However, the burning question in her mind was what the number on the license plate was going to be.

In a normal everyday conversation Grace typically asked a stream of questions that seemed to be insignificant and somewhat random. At times responding to all of them was exhausting for those around her. However, it wasn't until she was questioned further one day that it became evident that there was a clear purpose to her questions, albeit only to her. One afternoon, for what appeared to be no reason, Grace asked her dad what time he ate lunch. It seemed to be the beginning of another string of non-related questions. He answered her as usual. However, something that day made him ask her why she wanted to know. She told him she wanted to know when he ate to see if he could go to lunch with her at school. More typically the conversation would have started with the question, "Can you have lunch with me at school?" To which her dad could have responded, "What time do you eat?" While many times the child's focus may be different, the end result they want to achieve can sometimes be the same. So often there is a reason for their actions, but unless we delve deeper we may wrongly interpret their intent.

Understanding the way children with neurological differences think is the key to success in many areas. It is especially helpful, when you set out to teach them, to understand that their strengths in facts, details, and logic can be used as an advantage. Before Joshua had a specific diagnosis, I figured out that in order to teach him anything, I had to break the task into small steps. I remember teaching him how to tie his shoes. This was an arduous task. We would isolate a small part in the process, such as crossing the laces, by practicing just this step repeatedly until he got it. It was only then that we would add the next step in the sequence, careful to always start with step one. Somewhere along the line, I realized that if I wanted to teach him something this was the system that would give me the best chance for success.

So many times what works for these children goes against the norm of what society encourages parents to do. Early on as parents, you are bombarded with information discouraging parents from having their children watch television. I remember making a conscious effort to limit the amount of exposure Joshua had until I realized that for him it was an essential teaching tool. When Joshua was two, a speech therapist suggested certain television shows might be especially beneficial for him. That was a surprise for me, but it proved to be quite visionary. Over the years, I saw how much he learned from watching television—from learning to read, to understanding humor, emotions, and social situations. Consequently, I have learned to pick specific shows that can be of benefit because they match his developmental needs. After reading much of the current literature, I have found that I am not alone in observing that these children often learn better from television than observing real life. Knowing that this medium proves effective for him, we have continued to use it as a teaching tool as the opportunity presents itself throughout the course of a normal day. As soon as Joshua could talk, he would use phrases and jokes as his own that he picked up from television. Amazingly, he often used them in the appropriate context. Before I realized what he was doing, I was astonished and hopeful when I would hear these little gems. Although these days I'm not as encouraged when I hear something he has lifted from television, I still find it amusing and use it as a learning opportunity by checking his understanding and discussing its real meaning.

As Joshua watches television, he focuses on specific details, missing the overall picture. Missing the big picture is a common occurrence, which impacts the child's understanding in so many different situations. In the early school years, their focus on details works to their advantage, as they are often early readers, good decoders, and great spellers. This is the beginning of looking too good. Unfortunately, by third or fourth grade, it becomes apparent to the savvy observer that while they are able to decipher words well above their grade level, their ability to understand and interpret the text is lagging. In first grade, Joshua was given an assignment to write a summary sentence after each chapter he read. It became glaringly apparent to me that he was unable to summarize, as he gave me every meticulous detail. I could see it wasn't a lack of effort. No matter what support I provided, he just could not do it. This has continued to be a problem through sixth grade. After reading an article about the life of Helen Keller, Joshua was assigned the task of picking out ten facts and circling the three most important, followed by a summary sentence. Needless to say, when it came to picking out the ten facts, Joshua was a star. The brightness of the star quickly began to fade, as he was unable to determine the most important facts. The light was totally extinguished when I read Joshua's summary sentence, which focused solely on the fact that the most important part of Helen Keller's life was that she could speak many languages.

Their inability to grasp the big picture impacts them not only academically, but socially as well. Potentially meaningful conversational topics are reduced to a never-ending journey through details, much to the listener's dismay. Other times, their continued focus on the unimportant causes them to miss vital details. For instance, in sixth grade, the vice-principal gathered the boys for a question-and-answer session to supplement their sex education unit. A parent of another student who attended told me that the focus of the discussion was on protection. Joshua was deeply affected by the content. As I was preparing to cautiously approach the discussion with him, it was clear that there was no need for alarm. He was more than happy to share all that he had learned—which amounted to nothing concerning protection, only a funny joke that had been told. For him, it's as if that session never occurred. He got details, just the wrong ones. (Note to self: add protection to the list of needed discussions.)

Children with neurological differences often look happy when they are not, appear to understand when they don't, and to further complicate the matter, can't always take a skill learned in one situation and apply it in another. Is it any wonder that so much of what they do is misunderstood? Joshua's inability to generalize was evident at a young age as he played with toys. On his second birthday, he received a three-tiered toy garage complete with its own set of cars. It entertained him for hours as he watched the cars roll down the ramp, around the levels, over and over and over again. It looked like a great toy until we realized at Joshua's insistence that this was the only way in which to play with it. Only those cars were to be run down that track. Each toy had a specific purpose and was only to be used for that purpose. Even now he is infuriated when his brothers use a soccer ball to play kickball. A soccer ball is only used to play soccer, according to Joshua. This inflexible thinking leads him to such frustration that not only is he unable to participate in the game—he has to totally remove himself from the situation.

Inability to generalize is another result of inflexible thinking. What the child learns in one situation can not be transferred to even a similar circumstance, much less one that bears no resemblance. Often this inability reinforces the thinking that their behavior is intentional and intended in a negative way. When we went out to dinner one evening, the waitress, having made a mistake initially with Joshua's order, returned, having corrected it. She placed Joshua's food down before him and he responded with, "That's better." Joshua's response could have been interpreted as unappreciative, giving the appearance that he is not the sweet boy that he is. This, of course, was not the case, as he was clearly very pleased with having his food served the "right" way. The surprising thing about this incident was that Joshua, in so many other circumstances, always politely says "thank you." For some reason, he has not transferred that skill to waitresses in restaurants. The inability to transfer skills serves to further diminish the belief that a real problem exists, and leads to the never-ending question from teachers and others, "Why is it they can do it here, but they can't do it there?" As you try to explain this, you quickly get the feeling that you are viewed as a parent who explains away your child's behavior with excuses.

Many times this is the case when you are faced with situations that require your child to effectively use cause-and-effect thinking. Their inability to use cause-and-effect thinking leads them to act out a situation in order to determine the outcome. While sitting at a cafeteria table at school, Grace pondered what might happen if she took her tray and rammed it into the one next to her. Most of us would be able to think through the chain reaction that was about to occur, but she couldn't. Therefore, the only viable alternative for her to understand the cause and effect of the situation, was to give it a try. As you can imagine, her spirit of experimentation was promptly met with detention. A typical onlooker would, of course, view this behavior as intentionally disruptive, certain that there could be no other purpose. Grace, on the other hand, was sitting in detention wondering why she was there, but secure in her findings that there was conclusive evidence to indicate that one tray hitting another effects a chain reaction. When asked why she did this, her response was, "I wanted to see what would happen." Cause-and-effect thinking is often too abstract for these children to comprehend. So, experimenting with real objects and people makes the learning concrete for them.

In attempting to manage the behavior of children with neurological differences, the typical behavior modification system of rewards and punishments is ineffective. The inflexible thinking as well as the inability to generalize associated with their disorder results in their inability to learn from past mistakes, which is why consequences are ineffective. Thus far, all the classrooms my children have been in come equipped with the standard behavior plan. They typically require a child to earn a specified number of points or stickers in a month based on a certain "good behavior." At the end of the month, those children who have earned a set number of points are invited to attend a good behavior celebration, while those who have fallen short are not permitted to participate. Sadly, Joshua has missed almost every good behavior party, each month of each year, for his entire school career. This has not provided much incentive for wanting to go to school. In fourth grade, as usual, Joshua did not receive the required points to be invited to the doughnut party; however, he was expected to attend and watch, which he did with his head on his desk, crying, and arms covering his head. The note that came home explaining this stated, "I really wasn't picking on him. I hope he understands this is the outcome of reading during lessons, which he does most often to move his clip. (Joshua's clip is part of the class discipline/behavior program; each child in the class is given a clip, similar to a clothes-pin or a snack bag clip, which is moved by the teacher to a different level to signal to the child that their behavior is unacceptable.) It was obvious to me, he did not understand. While his unwanted behavior may have been pointed out, I don't believe it was ever accompanied by an explanation of why this was a problem and what to do instead. However, what I did understand was that his anxiety increased to the point of getting physically ill, knowing that he would assuredly miss the party. It seems to me that if the same children are missing the doughnut party every month, the behavior of these children is unchanged, rendering the plan ineffective. Although it is not always possible, the closer you can get to determining what they're thinking, the better off everybody involved will be. There is no question that you can punish endlessly, but in the end, what is required is a logical explanation accompanied by a description of what to do instead.

Their rigidity in thinking, language, and actions often leads to children with neurological differences being viewed as arrogant, controlling, and per-fectionistic. In their mind, there is only one right way, their way. They love being first in line and thinking they are the best in everything, while losing and criticism are very frustrating and hard for them to handle. Their inability to think flexibly can lead to upset for all involved. They can't understand what you want them to do or why, while you can't figure out a way to explain it so they can understand it. This is one more aspect of the disorder that requires an inor-dinate amount of energy, patience, and understanding.

Knowing about mental flexiblity helps you to accept those behaviors that are resistant to change and better understand some of the behaviors you would have previously found unacceptable. What would have driven you crazy before, now can even be viewed as endearing. As situations arise, you are better equipped to pick your battles, deciding whether to address it and explain, or accept it and enjoy who they are at that moment in time. Understanding the impact that lack of mental flexibility has on their behavior can go a long way towards improving the quality of life for all involved.

Things to consider

- Use the child's strengths to teach—detail-oriented, factual, logical.

- If a question the child asks seems meaningless, probe further to see what the child is thinking.

- Explain, explain, explain the why of everything.

- Talk to the child about what is important to know, understand, or do, and why.

- Don't expect the child to know how to apply acquired knowledge or skills to a new situation.

- As you watch television, or movies, or read, discuss the big ideas the writer might want to communicate.

- Talk to the child about what neurotypicals think is important and why. (Unfortunately, the why won't always make sense.)

- Try to make abstract concepts as concrete as possible by describing how they look and sound—when someone tells you to listen, that means to look at the person, sit quietly, don't move, etc.

- Help the child select the "important" information when they are required to summarize, explain, provide the main idea to complete school work, or in a conversation. Provide them with graphic organizers and strategies.

- Help the child work in groups to facilitate interactions and understand their role, so they don't appear bossy and perfectionistic.

Mental flexibility—STAT Example 10.1

Step 1: Assess the situation

In fourth grade, Joshua's teacher called home to let me know she was having trouble getting him to understand estimating. She said the class was given a list of numbers they were supposed to estimate in a given amount of time. She said that Joshua refused to estimate and instead added them up correctly in the allotted amount of time. When she spoke with him about it in the hallway, he said, "My Mom won't be proud of me if I don't get the right answer."

Step 2: Develop a hypothesis

Why? Why did they react the way they did? What could they be thinking? Select one or more of the elements below.

• Abstract language	• Motor	• Sensory	• Spatial orientation
• Control/ consistency	• Thinking about others thinking	• Social communication	• Emotions
• Mental flexibility	• Impulsive	• Executive function	• Anxiety

Hypothesis about their thinking (take a guess)

"Why should I guess and possibly be wrong when I can figure out the exact answer and know I'm right."

Step 3 (optional): Ask questions to obtain a step-by-step account

[Not needed in this example]

 Revise hypothesis. Go back to Step 2

Step 4: Actions to consider

Take action	**Seek additional sources of help**	• educators (teachers, aides, counselors, principal)
Take no action	• family members	• support professionals
Explain	• physician (change medication)	• parents of other children
Explain and take action	• neuropsychologist (further assessment)	• friends • community resources (social groups)

I explained to the teacher that Joshua sees things in black-and-white, right and wrong. There are no gray areas. In his mind, if he can get the exact answer, why guess and be wrong? For Joshua, it took many times of going over this concept, in many different ways, for him to be able to do it; however, I'm still not sure he really understands the purpose.

Additional comments

Initially, when Joshua "refused" to estimate, the teacher tried to illustrate the benefits by asking him to estimate a group of numbers that a student his age would not be able add in their head in the time provided. However, Joshua *was* able to add those numbers in that time frame, providing an exact and accurate answer. The teacher's attempt to highlight the benefits was lost on Joshua, and in fact reinforced his thinking that estimation served no purpose.

Based on the use of the word "refused," I assume the teacher perceived Joshua's actions as defiant behavior. However, if she had understood his lack of mental flexiblity was the result of his disorder, she could have viewed his behavior differently. She could have seen his thinking as logical, as opposed to mean-spirited. Realizing that he was unable to understand the benefits of estimation, she might have looked for a different way to present the information, and maybe even found some humor in the whole event.

Chapter 11

Impulsivity

**"The worst thing about NLD is when my mind tells me
to stop and my body won't listen"—Joshua.**

There he sat, once again reading a book while the other members of the class
were giving their presentations. As if this wasn't enough to agitate the teacher,
Joshua decided to participate, albeit in an inappropriate way. Just as one of the
little girls in the class was reaching the finale of her book presentation, Joshua
felt the urge to complete it for her. This was a major catastrophe for the girl,
made evident by her tears, and for the teacher, based on the note that came
home. Then again, everything was a major catastrophe for this particular
teacher. As I read the note, I felt a mix of emotions. I felt badly for the little girl
and even worse for Joshua that he had lost another potential friend without
understanding why. Although I had tried to explain Joshua's impulsivity to the
teacher on many occasions, she continued to view his behavior as a conscious
choice.

Once children with neurological deficit enter school, impulsive behavior
often becomes more of a problem due to the structured nature of the school
setting. The expected classroom behaviors, such as sitting quietly, raising your
hand, and carefully completing assignments, are in direct opposition to the way
their brain is wired. Because they are literally being asked to do something they
are incapable of, children with impulsivity issues begin to stick out when
compared with their peers. In today's society, there is a plethora of information
available about attention deficit hyperactivity disorder (ADHD) and impulsivity.

The majority of teachers have at least a basic understanding of what it is and what it looks like. Typically, a child with impulse control issues is able to express remorse at some point after they have been helped to realize the impact of their actions. The problem with children with nonverbal learning disorder (NLD), Asperger's, high-functioning autism (HFA), and pervasive developmental disorder-not otherwise specified (PDD-NOS) is that they have a theory of mind deficit coupled with an inability to control impulses. Why is this more of a problem, you might ask? When you have a theory of mind deficit, you are unable to understand the effects your actions may have had on someone else and, therefore, show no remorse. Back to the classroom incident, there stood the teacher with the little girl crying, and Joshua calmly returning to reading his book, totally unaffected by the upset his actions had caused. If he had only had the ability to understand how badly that little girl felt, coupled with the skills to apologize and make amends, the teacher would have viewed him differently. As it was, he appeared uncaring and cold, as if his actions were intentionally mean-spirited. As a teacher, if you believe the behavior to be a choice from a child showing no remorse, your frustration leads you to think negative conse-quences or punishment is the best option. However, in this case, what Joshua needed was an explanation of how his actions had impacted the girl. In addition, he also needed help to provide an apology in an attempt to repair the relationship. In Joshua's mind, the way it was left, he shared his knowledge with his classmates and somehow got in trouble. Another bad outcome for him, and another learning opportunity lost.

Blurting out answers is a common behavior in children lacking impulse control. It has been a recurrent issue for Joshua throughout his school career. I can't tell you how many notes have come home saying, "Josh is quick to show a classmate an answer," "Josh still struggles to raise his hand and wait to be called upon before speaking," "Josh is so anxious to give *all* answers he can hardly allow anyone else to give an answer." One teacher expressed what I believe was the feeling of most when she wrote, "I feel Josh is very aware of what is expected of him." For years, teachers worked on this unsuccessfully, until fourth grade, when we developed a card to be given to Joshua once he began to blurt out comments or answers.

When I really want to say something in class

- raise my hand
- wait for my turn to be called on
- if the teacher calls on someone else, it's okay
- listen to others' answers, the teacher will know I know the answer because I raised my hand
- be quiet but determined.

This proved to be successful because it curbed his impulse by providing him with a system describing what the appropriate behavior looked like. In addition, it addressed the purpose for his behavior, which was his need to let the teacher know how smart he was.

Impulsive children like to answer, but the ability to wait and think through a response is often lacking. When a question is asked, the first connection that comes to their mind comes out of their mouth. This becomes problematic because they impulsively draw conclusions that may be incorrect. However, if they had the ability to hold back and think about the topic, they would be able to make deeper connections. The impulsivity makes them unable to take the time needed to consider all aspects of a question or problem posed. This can be a problem academically across the board because it can lead to a false perception of their abilities. So often with these children, if you pursue their thinking with guiding questions, it becomes apparent that they know so much more than their original answer indicated. Of course, their developmental level in the areas of theory of mind, emotions, mental flexibility, and social communication needs to be considered when determining the depth of the connections they are able to make.

Talking before thinking creates problems academically, but also has a poten-tially negative effect socially. Comments have a tendency to spill out of their mouths, causing immediate damage that would be hard to repair if they only knew how. Grace was playing with her friend Abby when a recent a trip to a lake came up in conversation. Grace's mother commented that it would be nice if Abby joined them on next year's trip. Grace immediately responded, "I want Nicole to go again!" Assuming Abby's feelings would be hurt by the comment,

Grace's mother quickly turned to Grace with a facial expression highlighting the need for damage control. Seeing that Grace was oblivious, her mother quickly intervened in an attempt repair the damage. A child with impulse issues alone would probably have picked up on the social cues and been able to repair the situation. However, when combined with deficits in theory of mind and social communication, you don't know that you hurt someone's feelings, much less know how to go about fixing it.

Another recurring problem at school for children with control problems is their need to rush through classroom assignments. Once again, the notes from teachers start to roll in with consistent statements such as: "Josh rushes through his work so he can read," "Rushes through class work to get to other things." This need to complete things quickly is observed at home as well, because he wants to allot as much time as possible to those activities that he deems more appropriate. After all, he has his priorities. They just don't always coincide with the authorities in his world.

The lack of impulse control also makes it difficult for these children to wait. This can be a problem, as so much in our world requires us to wait. Think for a moment about how many places you find yourself having to wait, such as the doctor's office, amusement parks, restaurants, grocery store, school, concerts, plays, church, pretty much everywhere. Times like these are prime for meltdowns and other problems to occur. As you do with young children, the best you can do is anticipate problem situations and try to keep wait times to a minimum, engaging the child in other activities to take their mind off of it whenever possible. For me, when Joshua's brothers are involved, I naturally rely on that old standby of positioning myself as the buffer between him and them, as he commonly views poking them as an acceptable "other activity."

Sometimes, it's not just waiting in line or for your turn. Sometimes, it's waiting for an event. For Joshua, the time leading up to holidays, vacations, or his birthday are so full of anticipation. Along with this excitement, special events make the environment less consistent, increasing anxiety compromising his ability to control his impulses in many situations. I have learned to become much more cognizant of the calendar in relation to his behavior. Understanding this helps me to accept and plan for the change in his behavior: once I see that Joshua's impulses are becoming harder for him to control, I adjust the demands placed on him as best I can. However, by the time an important day arrives, it's all about damage control, because he has none. This was never more evident than on Christmas morning as he pushed past his brothers to get to the Christmas tree with no regard for anyone's safety. Now, each Christmas morning, I am prepared. As I see him coming down the hall, I greet him with a big hug that is sustained for an unusually long time, just enough to be sure the other boys make it safely down the stairs.

While waiting is difficult for these children, many times the same holds true for those around them, who find it hard to wait for them to stop. Joshua's brothers find his inability to stop when they ask, to be a recurring problem area. Many times a day I'm met with the words, "Mom, Josh won't stop…" It's easy to understand their frustration. Typically it begins with a fun, interactive, physical exchange that over time escalates, leaving everyone upset. While there are so many stories to choose from, I clearly remember the day Danny and Michael entered the house soaking wet. The two of them were dripping from head to toe, complaining, while Joshua happily entered a few steps behind with a few wet spots on his shirt. As everyone started talking at once, I was able to sort out that Michael had squirted Joshua with a squirt gun three times. Not to be outdone, Joshua retaliated—unfortunately, not in kind. The underlying theme was that what had started out in fun ended up as yet another problem, as Joshua refused to stop as requested when his two brothers had had enough.

Situations such as these also arise in the school setting. When you are asked to stop what you are doing, by either a teacher or a classmate, and you don't, your social standing takes a hit. It is certainly not the way to win friends or impress a teacher. I'm usually awarded the opportunity to participate in these situations, as this perceived refusal results in notes or phone calls home with the expectation of a remedy that I only wish I could provide. One of these memorable events occurred in fifth grade science class. A note came home indicating that during the process of dissecting owl pellets, Joshua repeatedly flicked his tweezers at his lab partner. His lab partner had asked him to stop several times, particularly upset as the tweezers had already been used in the owl pellets. Because Joshua didn't stop, she proceeded to tell the teacher, prompting the note. Again, what had the potential to be a positive social interaction ended badly for him, due to his lack of impulse control. In both situations, it wasn't what he did, it was that he did it to excess, once again missing the social cues and lacking the ability to think about others thinking.

The inability to think about the consequences of an action is the common thread present in the problem of impulsivity. This over-arching problem causes the blurting out, rushing through, acting before thinking, and waiting difficulties. Impulse control is a result of brain function and development which determines the ability of neurotypical children to control their actions. Again, it's often difficult to believe that a child who seems old enough to have that impulse control just doesn't. Their actions are not a choice; therefore, once again, discipline will prove to be ineffective. In that impulsive moment, try to work through it as safely and effectively as possible, waiting for a calmer time to explain what occurred, the emotional and physical effect on others, and what to do instead.

Things to consider

- Keep in mind that the child can't help it.
- Being patient will lessen the effect.
- At anxiety-provoking times, try to decrease demands and expectations placed on the child.
- Consider the pros and cons of medication, making decisions based on the unique needs of your child.
- For persistent, recurrent impulse-related problems, such as blurting out answers, consider strategies to deter impulsive reactions, such as reminder card.
- Educators might consider phrasing questions more specifically, e.g. instead of "Who knows the answer to…" say, "If you know the answer, raise your hand."

Impulsivity—STAT Example 11.1

Step 1: Assess the situation

On Christmas morning, Joshua would run to the presents, feverishly ripping the wrapping off of each gift, whether the gifts were his or not. He went through them one after the other in a matter of minutes, without really looking at or enjoying them. No one else in the family was able to enjoy the moment, as Joshua made it so frenetic and chaotic.

Step 2: Develop a hypothesis

Why? Why did they react the way they did? What could they be thinking? Select one or more of the elements below.

• Abstract language	• Motor	• Sensory	• Spatial orientation
• Control/ consistency	• Thinking about others thinking	• Social communication	• Emotions
• Mental flexibility	• Impulsive	• Executive function	• Anxiety

Hypothesis about their thinking (take a guess)

What could they be thinking to themselves? What would they be saying?

"I can't wait to open these presents!"

↓

Step 3 (optional): Ask questions to obtain a step-by-step account

Types of questions

[Not needed in this example]

↓ ↳ Revise hypothesis. Go back to Step 2 ↑

Step 4: Actions to consider

Take action	Seek additional sources of help	• educators (teachers, aides, counselors, principal)
Take no action	• family members	• support professionals
	• physician (change medication)	• parents of other children
Explain		• friends
	• neuropsychologist (further assessment)	• community resources (social groups)
Explain and take action		

Instead of wrapping all the gifts, I decided to set out some unwrapped gifts for Joshua to focus on first, in an effort to help him release his initial excitement. I make sure to leave unwrapped the gift he has most anticipated, so he won't go through the wrapped gifts looking for it.

Additional comments

I realized early on that Joshua was not able to control this impulsive behavior, so I decided that I needed to change the way the gifts were presented in order for the rest of the family to be able to enjoy the events. Although it isn't the way I envisioned Christmas morning, this made it manageable and more enjoyable.

It's not unusual for younger children to engage in this type of behavior when receiving gifts, as impulse control is developmental. However, in Joshua's case, this behavior has continued, improving little with age.

Impulsivity—STAT Example 11.2

Step 1: Assess the situation

Grace's parents pull up to school expecting to attend a basketball game, and instead see fire trucks. They were hopeful Grace and the fire trucks were not linked. They were met at the door by the principal, who informed them that Grace had set off the sprinkler system by igniting a lighter under one.

↓

Step 2: Develop a hypothesis

Why? Why did they react the way they did? What could they be thinking? Select one or more of the elements below.

• Abstract language	• Motor	• Sensory	• Spatial orientation
• Control/ consistency	• Thinking about others thinking	• Social communication	• Emotions
• Mental flexibility	• Impulsive	• Executive function	• Anxiety

Hypothesis about their thinking (take a guess)

"Would that be enough fire to set it off?"

↓

Step 3 (optional): Ask questions to obtain a step-by-step account

Types of questions

[Not needed in this example]

↓↳ Revise hypothesis. Go back to Step 2

Step 4: Actions to consider		
Take action	**Seek additional sources of help**	• educators (teachers, aides, counselors, principal)
Take no action	• family members	• support professionals
	• physician (change medication)	• parents of other children
Explain		• friends
	• neuropsychologist (further assessment)	• community resources (social groups)
Explain and take action		

Take action by paying the fine issued by the fire department. Explain, to Grace, the other options available for finding out answers to her questions.

Additional comments

As the consequences of her actions never crossed her mind, Grace impulsively went forward with her experiment. Grace did not have the mental flexibility to determine the cause and effect of her actions, as she could not abstractly think it through without actually doing it.

Chapter 12

Executive Functions

"I got your note in Joshua's planner concerning his missing assignments"—note to the teacher from Joshua's mother.

Tissues. It might be hard to believe that tissues could tell a story, but these particular tissues spoke volumes. On the last day of sixth grade, Joshua came home with four unopened boxes of tissues that appeared to be the same ones that had been requested by each of the classroom teachers at the beginning of the year. However, these tissue boxes did not look exactly like the ones I sent in, as they were smashed and misshapen, indicating the trauma they had endured. When I asked Joshua why he had brought these home, he looked at me blankly and said, "I don't know, they were just in my locker." I thought about those tissues stacked on top of each other in Joshua's locker, all year long. I began to feel overwhelmed with emotion as I thought about him attempting to get books and binders in and out of his locker, all the time trying to maneuver around these boxes. At this moment these tissues told me that he probably hadn't, the entire school year, had the support I was sure was in place. Upset as that thought made me feel, I was equally discouraged to realize that Joshua didn't have the executive function skills necessary to see this as a problem, much less be able to find a solution.

Executive functions are part of our everyday life and are the skills we use to structure our day. Various authors have defined executive functions differently. For our purposes here, we are viewing executive functions as those skills that allow one to plan, sequence, organize, prioritize, and problem-solve in order to complete complex tasks. Different environments require different abilities in the area of executive functions. Success in the school and work environments are typically tied to your executive functioning abilities; while home and community environments are more forgiving of those who lack the skills in this area. At home, children have the built-in support of their parents to structure and prioritize the important events of their day. However, once they enter school, they are required to take on more of those tasks, and deficits become more apparent. As with all areas, children with neurological differences have executive function skills that span the continuum. Some children might have difficulty with sequencing daily hygiene tasks, such as brushing their teeth, while others may experience trouble only in the school arena with tasks requiring organizing and planning papers or projects.

Nothing seems to highlight difficulties with executive functioning more dramatically than the beginning of the school year. Parents make every attempt to help their children transition easily to the new school year. As I began to get my boys ready for this school year, I realized how different the preparation was for Joshua, compared to the other two. The differences are both physical and emotional for the children and me. In the case of Michael and Danny, there is minimal anxiety on my part in dealing with their concerns. Typically, they ask me questions about their worries, I provide an answer, and we come up with a plan that relieves their anxiety. For instance, this year, Michael, who is eight, asked how he would know where to go when he got off the bus. I provided simple directions to his class and told him Danny would walk him there the first day. Michael's question was answered and all was well with the world.

Joshua, on the other hand, is a totally different story. When the calendar changes to the first day of August and we know school is fast approaching, his anxiety, and mine, rises to a new height. And so it begins. Aside from trying to manage his anxiety, I have to make special arrangements to get his schedule ahead of time. Once that is accomplished, I review it, attempting to think through every step he will take and the potential pitfalls he may encounter. Difficult as this can be, I realize how important it is, because Joshua is not able to complete this process on his own. Typically, someone his age would figure it out as they go, making adjustments where necessary. Joshua, on the other hand, due to his deficit in executive functions, is not able to find a solution to a problem, much less identify that one even exists.

The planning process begins once we acquire the schedule of classes. We schedule multiple sessions to walk through the building to rehearse his schedule. With schedule in hand, we begin with exiting the bus, entering the building, and walking through the entire schedule, including intermittent trips to his locker to retrieve and deposit books, until he is back on the bus. We go through his entire schedule exactly as he will go through it, and then we go through it again.

From there, organization is the next hurdle. We develop a system that will enable him to efficiently and effectively arrive at class on time with everything he will need. As we purchase the items on the supply list, Joshua's presence is necessary as I have him review and approve each item that will be purchased. I want to be sure before we buy an item that Joshua is comfortable with all aspects of it. For instance, Joshua prefers a certain type of highlighter, a specific mechanical pencil, and a binder that closes to his specifications. Needless to say, once I find an item that passes inspection, such as the pencils, I buy in bulk in case I am unable to find them again. Unbeknownst to him, I am sure some of his selections are based on sensory and motor issues.

Next, the color-coding begins. Each subject requires a folder with an individual color, accompanied by a matching book cover. Joshua needs to be able to quickly identify each folder from the outside. Understanding he might not be able to remember which color identifies each subject, it is on to labeling. This year my label maker and I spend much quality time together as I neatly label each folder in not just one, but two different places. Much to my dismay, I am compelled to start over as my husband, passing through the kitchen, noticed the labels. He thought the printed labels were not "cool" enough and might lead to teasing by the other children. Note to self: next year, check to see what the other children are doing before you start.

Each year brings different requirements, which, in turn, bring the need for a new system. This year, instead of one binder for all subjects, Joshua is required to have individual binders for each class. Thus, the dilemma of determining the logistics of his writing utensils. I know Joshua will never be able to remember which supplies he needs for each class. One class requires color pencils, one highlighters, another red pens, and on and on. At first, I thought I would put everything in one pencil pouch, but then I realized how big it would have to be and how easily that could lead to teasing. Finally, I settled on an individual pouch that fit in the binder for each subject. I'm sure next year will bring a new set of circumstances to work through.

All of this, and the school year hasn't even begun. While it seems the focus of this chapter thus far might be me instead of Joshua, I assure you that is not the case. The absence of Joshua's participation in the school preparation process indicates the severity of executive function deficits. There are few children who require this level of support at the age of twelve. Children with executive function deficits need someone to provide that consistency in order to give them the best chance to succeed. Most often, it's their mother who becomes the executive secretary, requiring a tremendous amount of thought, time, and effort. Many times, this is misinterpreted and viewed as unnecessary coddling. However, I can assure you that no one wants them to be independent more than the parent. Each year, Joshua has made progress in the amount of insight he can contribute to this process. I feel hopeful that he is making progress, as independence is the ultimate goal. However, as this progress is slow and incremental, it requires awareness and continuous monitoring of the skills he's gained, as well as those that still need to be supported.

The problems that arise once the school year begins are fairly consistent from year to year. Unfortunately, they seem to last throughout the year; somehow, no amount of planning eliminates them completely. The first, and never-ending, area of concern is the dreaded homework planner. I call it the "hieroglyphics" notebook. Sometimes, there is nothing there when there should be; sometimes there is something there that shouldn't be; but most of the time, there is just enough there so you're sure you need to do something, you just can't be certain what that might be. The interrogation of your child begins. It baffles me how a child who can rattle off the state capitals in alphabetical order, can't remember what he's supposed to do for math that day. Many nights, we have spent hours deciphering the information in the planner, trying to determine what needs to be completed for the next day. Unfortunately, this process often took longer than the completion of the homework. On those rare occasions when we were able to figure out what needed to be done, the next hurdle was determining if Joshua had happened to bring home the necessary books and materials to complete the task. It's not the act of finishing the homework that is the problem at our house. The problem is the preparation to determine what needs to be done, explaining this to Joshua, suggesting an order for completion, with built-in periodic checks for understanding, culminating with the process of preparing it for delivery the next day. It's important to be sure the homework is in the correct folder, but that does not always ensure it will make it to its final destination. Even then, I'm not surprised when a note comes home concerning a missing assignment. The executive functions involved in completing homework, planning, organizing, sequencing, prioritizing, and actually finishing the work, make the tasks surrounding the actual homework impossible to complete independently for someone with a deficit in this area. Neurotypical students are able to complete this homework preparation process with ease, as they employ their executive functions with minimal thought and effort.

Fortunately, Joshua has always had the ability to understand the academic subject matter. He understands the concepts and principles presented. However, his problems become evident when he is required to show what he knows in the format requested of him. His ability to complete the work is directly tied to the complexity of the task. The more complex the task requirements, the less likely he is to be able to demonstrate his understanding of the subject. Directions have been an ongoing problem. Multi-step directions are particularly troublesome. Typically, when given a set of directions, Joshua only responds to the first task, then thinks he's finished. This can have a negative impact on his grade, when in reality it's not the material he doesn't understand, it's the format. The same holds true when he is asked to complete projects or reports. The need to break a project into parts and determine how much time is required for each, taxes his executive function abilities. His sense of time has always seemed compromised, as until just recently he has had difficulty placing events in the time frame in which they occur. This always made problem situations difficult to deal with, as I could never be sure when the event he was relating actually happened.

Deficits in the areas of organization, planning, sequencing, and prioritizing all combine to make problem-solving difficult. Most of us automatically and unconsciously think through the steps of problems many times a day, never stopping to consider what is involved. To problem-solve, the first step is to identify the problem. Unfortunately, children with neurological differences struggle to perceive the presence of a problem, much less what it might actually be. It's encouraging to see Joshua begin to develop in this area. Even though he still needs assistance to resolve a problem, the fact that he is beginning to be able to identify a problem eliminates the guessing on my part and much of the anxiety on his. For instance, the night before seventh grade was to start, he approached me, worried about how to get his trombone to the band room and still be where he needed to be on time. It was a happy moment for me, as it's so much easier to deal with a problem when you know what it is, not to mention that it was a problem I hadn't thought of. Once the problem was identified, it was easy to work through the steps of determining his options and the consequences of each to identify his best option. Several years ago, this wouldn't have been possible, but this year he had the ability to provide input into the process, instead of me simply guessing and telling him what to do.

It's one thing to anticipate a problem, but dealing with one as it is occurring requires more developed problem-solving skills, as situations need to be assessed quickly. These types of problems present themselves daily for all of us and are usually easily dealt with. However, for children with a neurological difference, simple problems can escalate into much larger ones because they lack the ability to address them. In fourth grade, Joshua sat in his classroom attempting to locate the folder he needed. As all his folders were combined into one larger binder, he simply placed the entire binder on his desk and opened it, oblivious to the fact that one fourth of it would end up on his classmate's desk. His classmate indicated her objection to this intrusion. However, Joshua, unable to determine a solution that would be a win for both of them, chose to do nothing. Obviously, this didn't work for her, which lead to him being subjected to the teacher's ire for being the cause of this disruption. Once again, Joshua found himself in a situation where he was in trouble without knowing why. If he had only had the problem-solving skills to take the folder out of the binder to begin with, it would have resulted in one less upset in his day.

People's ability to use their executive functions, break down complicated tasks, and problem-solve are used with such ease on a daily basis, that it is difficult to consider that someone may not be able to do the same. Once you understand that children's responses may be, in part, due to difficulty in these areas, you are in a position to help. As with so many other areas, you want to provide the level of support they need, while at the same time helping them to develop the skills they are lacking. Providing the needed support, especially in school, is essential if these children are going to be able to show what they truly do know. Progress may be slow and incremental, but it does happen. Executive function skills allow us to operate in an organized manner, giving life order. By helping them to make sense out of the chaos, you provide an environment in which living and learning have a chance to take place.

Things to consider

- Make necessary accommodations. Determine if the child's ability to show what they know is being compromised.

- Constantly monitor tasks providing scaffolded support. You model the task, do it together, and then they try it by themselves.

- Help them prioritize tasks and long-term projects, providing a reasonable time for completion.

- Chunk information into smaller bits.

- Provide strategies and supports in the way of graphic organizers, lists, etc.

- Think aloud as you problem-solve situations, so that the child can hear the process of your thinking.

- Visually display the steps of problem-solving in an easily accessible place, so that as problems arise you can use them to look at options and alternatives.

- Remember that inability to problem-solve can be impacted or have impact on the other deficit areas.

Executive functions—STAT Example 12.1

Step 1: Assess the situation
On several consecutive evenings, I found a pile of soaking wet towels in the bathroom after Joshua finished his bedtime routine.

Step 2: Develop a hypothesis

Why? Why did they react the way they did? What could they be thinking? Select one or more of the elements below.

• Abstract language	• Motor	• Sensory	• Spatial orientation
• Control/ consistency	• Thinking about others thinking	• Social communication	• Emotions
• Mental flexibility	• Impulsive	• Executive function	• Anxiety

Hypothesis about their thinking (take a guess)

I couldn't come up with a possible explanation.

Step 3 (optional): Ask questions to obtain a step-by-step account

Types of questions

"Why am I finding these extremely wet towels on the bathroom floor every night?" **"I'm trying to clean up the bubbles in the sink."** "Why are there bubbles in the sink?" **"From when I wash my hands."** Realizing he was using to much soap, I asked him how many times he pushed the soap pump. **"Three."**

 Revise hypothesis. Go back to Step 2

Step 2: Develop a hypothesis

Why? Why did they react the way they did? What could they be thinking? Select one or more of the elements below.

• Abstract language	• Motor	• Sensory	• Spatial orientation
• Control/ consistency	• Thinking about others thinking	• Social communication	• Emotions
• Mental flexibility	• Impulsive	• Executive function	• Anxiety

Hypothesis about their thinking (take a guess)

"There are too many bubbles in this sink. I need to clean this up so I'll use these towels."

Step 4: Actions to consider		
Take action	**Seek additional sources of help**	• educators (teachers, aides, counselors, principal)
Take no action	• family members	• support professionals
	• physician (change medication)	• parents of other children
Explain		• friends
	• neuropsychologist (further assessment)	• community resources (social groups)
Explain and take action		

I explained that the bubbles were caused by too much soap. He only needed to push the pump once to get the amount of soap he needed.

Additional comments

Joshua did come up with a solution to his problem, although it didn't address the cause. Joshua was unable to problem-solve that the cause of too many bubbles was too much soap. The problem was easily resolved with a simple explanation. This story illustrates how an executive function deficit can impact the daily lives of children and their families.

Chapter 13

Anxiety

"It's best just to let him call home when he wants"
—comment made at meeting to introduce Joshua to
new team members, by an educational team member
familiar with him.

It was a morning just like any other morning. Joshua had been at school for a few hours, I hadn't as yet received any phone calls. I'm thinking I'm going to have a good day. Not so fast. I unsuspectingly open my email, only to find I have a sauce problem. Although there was no mention of the word "irritated," the tone came through loud and clear. Joshua's support educator expressed an urgent need for me to impart to Joshua that he would indeed be able to have his sauce on the side. As I read on, I realized she was referring to an upcoming sixth grade class field trip that included lunch at an Italian restaurant. I could just see it. Joshua moving from teacher to teacher asking for assurance that he could get his spaghetti sauce on the side, until finally they could take it no more. When Joshua got home that day, I happily delivered the good news that it would be possible for him to receive his sauce on the side. As he exhaled deeply, you could almost see the anxiety leave his body. All this upset over sauce on the side.

It seems so trivial, yet for him it was a major anxiety-provoking situation. So often the worries of children with neurological differences are dismissed as insignificant, which only serves to compound the problem. What happened in this case is a perfect example of something that could have been easily remedied instead of escalating. Since no one that he consulted felt the same urgency he did, he didn't get a response, and therefore this remained his sole focus, gaining momentum and resulting in a problem for everyone. It could have been as easy as, "Sure, Josh, we'll take care of that." It's not about what others deem as worthy of concern; it's about the child's perception of a situation and the resulting anxiety. The bottom line is that if you don't address their anxiety, the problem you judged to be insignificant will be yours shortly.

Anxiety is a constant in the world of a child diagnosed with a neurological disorder. They live in a world that is confusing and frightening because they can never be sure how to interpret or respond to the world around them. When you face a world each day where each action has the potential for disaster, how could you not feel anxiety? For most people, anxiety is part of life that periodically occurs and can often serve a productive purpose. However, to be in a constant state of anxiety is mentally and physically unhealthy. Anxiety levels are different for each child; however, with some children with these differences, the anxiety can be so intense that it has a significant impact on their ability to participate in various aspects of society. Different children fall into different places on the anxiety continuum. For instance, Grace and her mother could often be seen sitting in their car outside school, trying to relieve Grace's anxiety enough for her to get in the door. For some children, this would be a typical first day of school occurrence, but for Grace this lasted for the entire year, never seeming to improve. Anxiety is an individualized response. Just as the degree of anxiety is different for each child, so is the cause. There is no specific formula for diagnosing the cause of the anxiety or the extent to which the child will be affected by it.

Each child expresses and deals with their anxiety in different ways. It's the job of parents and professionals to be familiar with and acknowledge the indicators specific to each individual child. Anxiety indicators as we define them are the behaviors the child exhibits to indicate there is a problem. These behaviors are flags to the parent, requiring some action to be taken. If left unattended, the anxiety and accompanying behavior will continue to escalate. Spotting the presence of these behaviors can be difficult, as some are subtle while others blatant. So often in the presence of a problem, these children have great difficulty identifying their emotions, as well as expressing their worries. Consequently, indicators can be used to your advantage because they communicate the need for help on the part of the child. Anxiety indicators take many forms. For Grace, twirling, physically spinning in circles, was a big one. While she frequently twirled to get sensory input, adults who interacted with Grace knew that when the twirling intensified, she was basically holding up a sign that said,

"I have a problem. I'm anxious. Help me." Grace's twirling made it easy to identify that there was a problem. For Joshua, one of his indicators is talking to himself. When I watch him get off the bus and walk down the driveway, if I see his mouth moving a mile a minute, I know something's up. Both of these behaviors are beneficial, as they can be used as tools that indicate something is wrong, even if you don't know what it is. The more adept you are at seeing the indicators, the more successful you are at minimizing the associated anxiety.

When you are aware of the presence of a problem, your odds of fixing it greatly increase. The scary part is when you find out that there has been an ongoing one that you knew nothing about. Through the first four years of elementary school, Joshua had casually mentioned, on numerous occasions, a kid who seemed to rub him the wrong way. Not that he used those exact words, as he would be clueless to the meaning. Come to find out, this boy had been bullying Joshua all along. The culmination came in fourth grade when he would walk by Joshua in class and say, "You're a dead man at recess." Now, while this statement in and of itself is bad enough, when taken literally, as Joshua did, it compounds the problem. Joshua really and truly believed there was a possibility he might be killed at recess. Unbelievable as this sounds, that is the reality in which he lived. Not until summertime, by complete accident, was I able to get enough pieces of the puzzle to put together the situation and its ramifications. As there were no obvious signs indicating the presence of a problem, it basically went unaddressed, relegating him to four years of constant fear.

In fourth grade Joshua's anxiety peaked, providing many examples of the different forms anxiety can take. He had no diagnosis, no IEP (Individual Education Plan), no belief on the part of the educational system, and no support. Joshua's nightly schedule seemed to be get ready for bed, throw up, go to bed and try to go to sleep. I started to track on a calendar each time he threw up, and to my surprise, his vomiting experience occurred Sunday through Thursday like clockwork. Being the detective I am, I quickly determined there was a direct correlation between going to school and vomiting. Until this point, the upset was all-consuming for the entire household because Joshua was unable to communicate his feelings. Currently, in seventh grade, it's music to my ears when Joshua is able to say, "My stomach feels funny and I don't know why," as this automatically indicates to me the presence of a fairly serious problem that needs to be addressed.

As I look back, I realize how much progress has been made in controlling Joshua's anxiety and allowing him to function to his fullest potential. Each year prior to the first day of school, as I meet with Joshua's team of teachers, the one message I want to convey clearly is the need to keep his anxiety to a minimum. The lower his anxiety, the closer to normal he is able to function. As his anxiety increases, his ability to function in other areas decreases, leading to a multitude of problems. The next step is to explain what needs to happen to keep his anxiety low. One of the most critical components, for him, is for everyone involved in his school day to understand that he needs caring assurance, acceptance, and the knowledge that if and when he makes a mistake, he will not be in trouble. Many of these children have what we'll term check phrases. These are phrases children use repeatedly to make sure they are safe and secure in the present situation. Joshua's phrase is "Am I in trouble?" Grace uses "Are you mad at me?" and "I'm okay?" These phrases are requests made to adults to obtain an expression of reassurance. If you are unsure of when you've made a mistake, it makes sense to check regularly to see if you have. Therefore, for Joshua, I start many conversations with, "You're not in trouble." Otherwise, I can be sure his anxiety will prevent him from hearing what I need him to hear.

In addition, part of Joshua's anxiety reduction plan includes having a "safe person" to go to at any point during the day when he feels the need. Normally, this distinction falls to the support educator because she is knowledgeable about his IEP, my main contact, and acts as the intermediary to resolve any concerns that arise with the teachers. Out of all this, all Joshua cares about is that he has a safe place to go and someone who can help him. It's also necessary that the plan include that Joshua has permission to call home whenever he feels it necessary. This serves a couple of purposes. First, just having contact with me relieves his anxiety. Second, it allows me to gain insight into a possible explanation for his increased anxiety, as it is not always obvious or simple to ascertain. The accommodation that has had the biggest impact in reducing Joshua's anxiety has been the substitution of a problem-solving plan for detention. In the past, the mere mention of the word would send Joshua's anxiety levels soaring, causing him to become unable to function, and so almost assuring him a place in detention. Detention can be a sticky subject in schools. Behavior that would warrant detention should be intentional. However, in the case of these children, so much of their inappropriate behavior is unintentional, therefore detention will have no impact in changing the behavior. The substitution of a problem-solving plan teaches them what to do instead. In Joshua's case, once detention was not a threat, he felt such relief that he no longer had to consider that possibility, and those situations that would have landed him in detention were avoided. For instance, if Joshua thought he were going to get detention for being late to class, his anxiety level would escalate, making him unable to open his locker and quickly select the appropriate materials that he needed. This, of course, would result in him being late for class. Eliminating detention eliminated the anxiety, which eliminated being late for class, and the need for detention. What a vicious cycle!

When these children get the feeling that they are out of favor with certain people in their everyday lives, they begin to make an extra effort to try and please them. Knowing someone doesn't like them makes them anxious, causing them to try to repair the damage even though they're not sure what the damage is. With limited social skills, this attempt at damage control is often futile and only serves to make the individual they are trying to please react in a negative manner. The more they try, the worse it gets. As their anxiety increases, their attempts to fix the situation increase proportionally. Grace was unable to interpret the communication style of a particular teacher at her school. As a result, she wasn't able to receive the feedback being given that would have shown her that the teacher liked her, which caused her anxiety to escalate. In an attempt to connect with this teacher, Grace intently focused her efforts on being anywhere and everywhere this teacher was. She constantly interjected herself into this teacher's social situations, as if she was on a mission. Unfortunately, the more effort she made to connect, the more annoying she became. The perception of not pleasing an adult or sensing that an adult is not pleased with you causes great anxiety, resulting in an attempt to correct the situation—unfortunately with the use of often inappropriate social skills. This, in turn, leads to an adult who is not pleased with you. Another vicious cycle!

When the life you live is one of constant anxiety, breaks become an essential component for survival. Anxiety causes stress and tension at an unconscious level, resulting in physiological changes. To live in a world of constant anxiety is unhealthy. Although children with neurological differences may not consciously understand the need for a break, they sometimes attempt unknowingly to build them in on their own. After receiving yet another friendly correspondence from school before Joshua's IEP was in place, I realized Joshua had found a way to provide himself with relief in an acceptable way. The note read, "Josh enjoys going to the bathroom and getting a drink. He likes the freedoms. I mentioned his 3–4 trips per class period (two hours) will need to end as we begin our testing." Although I don't think Joshua realized at a conscious level that he needed a break from the stress of the class, I do think he understood he felt better. I visualized him stepping into the hallway breathing a deep sigh of relief, almost able to see the tension leaving his body. While I saw it as a positive and necessary tactic, his teacher, I believe, viewed it as a misuse of a privilege. The note that came home the following week supported my thinking as it stated, "Josh has been able to complete tests without needing a bathroom break. Who knew he could stay in one room for 2–2½ hours without going to the restroom." As I thought about it, taking a test requires practically no social interaction, leaving little chance for error and teacher disapproval. How sad is it that a testing situation was less stressful for Joshua than a typical school day.

Breaks are a natural part of everybody's day. However, for the child with neurological differences, breaks are essential, often solitary, and longer in length. This often becomes a dilemma for parents at home, as they try to balance the amount of social time with the child's need for solitary time. You know they need both, but how much, is the question. In Joshua's case, these solitary times are a necessary part of his day that I make a conscious effort to accommodate. When planning our family's schedule, I make every attempt not to overschedule Joshua's day. For him, that means no more than one required event in addition to school. A trombone lesson and a haircut on the same day would be totally out of the question. On those rare, unavoidable occasions, his anxiety starts the minute he knows, worrying that his requirement for alone time won't be met. Joshua is in such a state of upset that he can't think of anything else, and is relentless in his expression of his misery. Even when that day has ended, it's not over. His upset continues on affecting the plans of the next day. It is better for all of us if he gets his time. In his case, it's not just a want; it's a need.

It's easy to understand the need for solitary time when you consider this simple equation that governs the child's existence: people = social = anxiety = exhaustion = meltdowns. While it is not feasible or preferable for them to live in solitude, it is important to have social circles of acceptance built into their lives. These are groups of people who have consistently provided an environment for safe interactions. They can be family, extended family, family friends, and peers. Social interaction with these groups is as anxiety-free as possible, providing an atmosphere in which the child can learn to use social skills without negative reaction. Families do this naturally, but at school it can be helpful to orchestrate these environments for your child to ensure some supported social interaction. For instance, at the beginning of every year, we try to make sure Joshua has specific peers to eat lunch with who have proven to be kind and open to the possibility of a friendship. This provides support and structure to the only part of his day where there typically isn't any. This situation is not as anxiety-free as a family one, but it's certainly much less stressful than being left to navigate on his own. Social circles of acceptance provide an environment that is safe, caring, and supportive.

Anxiety issues get complicated due to lack of development in the other deficit areas. When they overlap, things get muddied and getting to the root of the anxiety becomes more difficult. One day when I was accompanying Joshua to an ophthalmology appointment, several deficit areas overlapped at the same time in the same moment, creating one of those visual memories never to be forgotten. As the nurse put drops in Joshua's eyes, he had what others would view as an exaggerated reaction to the burning sensation he felt. As the nurse began to apply the second round of drops, he asked her if these would burn too. She said, "No, because I just numbed your eyes." Instantly, his legs went straight out, becoming totally stiff. He grabbed the arms of the chair with a panicked look on his face. Joshua and I then moved to another room to wait for the drops to take effect. As I saw the tears form in his eyes, I told him not to cry or the drops would come out and they would have to do it again. He put his head on my shoulder, pitifully asking, "Is this legal?" Talk about a smorgasbord of deficit areas. First, there was the sensory issue of dealing with the hypersensitive reaction to the drops. Next, the language issue of his inability to understand the term "numb." Then, his inability to identify his emotions, coupled with his undeveloped social communication skills to explain his state of mind. It's easier to address a situation once you are aware of where it is all coming from. By taking into consideration the combination of contributing factors, it became possible to minimize the effects of his anxiety, making a bad situation just a little bit better.

Understanding the enormity of the child's anxiety is essential if you are going to truly help them. Unfortunately, this seems to be the hardest area for people to see and therefore believe. Of all the areas listed on the STAT, anxiety is the one that needs to be addressed first. Unless anxiety is addressed and at least minimized, the child will be unable to deal cognitively with any of the other areas. This seems so complicated when you consider their anxiety actually results from their neurological differences in all the other areas on the STAT. Nevertheless, it's important to remember that anxiety is a part of their life every day, impacting everywhere they go and everything they do. What may seem insignificant to you is real to them. Minimizing or ignoring it is a huge mistake. The saddest thing to consider is the possibility of suicide that can be the result of a life filled with anxiety. The statistics seem to indicate that the incidence of suicide by individuals diagnosed with neurological differences is higher than in the typical population, and one can certainly understand why. It takes great courage to overcome the anxiety they are forced to face in the ambiguous world before them each day. Make every effort to make their life as anxiety-free as possible.

Things to consider

- Do whatever it takes to make the child feel safe and protected in their environment.

- Consider an alternative to the school discipline policy. Consider a problem-solving organizer instead of detention.

- Provide a safe person at school.

- Ask them frequently if they feel safe.

- Remember that threats and ultimatums in response to their behavior only serve to increase their anxiety… Teach what to do instead.

- Help them identify their anxiety and the physiological changes that occur as a result.

- Provide them with techniques to control their anxiety, such as relaxation exercises and cognitive behavior therapy.

- Let them know everyone feels anxious at times.

- Talk out loud about your anxiety—tell them how you feel and why.

- Don't dismiss their anxiety. It doesn't matter if the anxiety seems real or not to you, if it's real to them you need to address it.

Anxiety—STAT Example 13.1

Step 1: Assess the situation

In fifth grade, Joshua's support educator called me from school to tell me there had been a "shelter in place drill" that had appeared to upset Joshua. She explained that during the drill Joshua was the only child under a desk with a coat over his head.

Note: A "shelter in place drill" is like a tornado drill that children practice in schools in the event of other emergencies.

Step 2: Develop a hypothesis

Why? Why did they react the way they did? What could they be thinking? Select one or more of the elements below.

• Abstract language	• Motor	• Sensory	• Spatial orientation
• Control/ consistency	• Thinking about others thinking	• Social communication	• Emotions
• Mental flexibility	• Impulsive	• Executive function	• Anxiety

Hypothesis about their thinking (take a guess)

"I'm upset because there has been an unexpected change in my day." At this point, I thought Joshua's reaction indicated he was anxious due to the upset in his routine.

Step 3 (optional): Ask questions to obtain a step-by-step account

Types of questions

When Joshua came home from school, I asked him about the shelter in place drill. He said, **"It wasn't a drill. I was really scared. I put my jacket over my head and was shaking."**

 Revise hypothesis. Go back to Step 2

Step 2: Develop a hypothesis

Why? Why did they react the way they did? What could they be thinking? Select one or more of the elements below.

• Abstract language	• Motor	• Sensory	• Spatial orientation
• Control/ consistency	• Thinking about others thinking	• Social communication	• Emotions
• Mental flexibility	• Impulsive	• Executive function	• Anxiety

Hypothesis about their thinking (take a guess)

"Oh my gosh! I might die. I'm going to do everything I can to protect myself."

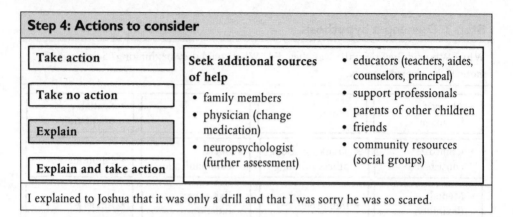

Step 4: Actions to consider		
Take action	Seek additional sources of help	• educators (teachers, aides, counselors, principal)
Take no action	• family members	• support professionals
	• physician (change medication)	• parents of other children
Explain		• friends
	• neuropsychologist (further assessment)	• community resources (social groups)
Explain and take action		

I explained to Joshua that it was only a drill and that I was sorry he was so scared.

Additional comments

Initially, I thought Joshua's reaction was mainly the result of a disruption in his schedule that was cause for some anxiety. However, after realizing that Joshua thought that there truly was a chemical spill, I realized that the cause for his atypical reaction was more anxiety than anything else. The control/consistency aspect of a changed routine played a lesser role. I was distraught about Joshua having to endure such fear and anxiety unnecessarily, because if he had just looked around at the other children he would have realized they were unaffected. This lack of mental flexibility contributed in large part to the increase in his anxiety.

Chapter 14

Believe

"I thought Joshua had problems with his heart, because that's where the love comes from" —Joshua's brother Michael, age seven.

Whoever thought getting in the car could be a contact sport. At my house, it is. We were getting ready to leave and, much to Joshua's dismay, he was not the first to arrive to claim his preferred seat. Danny had beaten him to it, relegating him to the back. Joshua, always first in the van, had pushed Danny, hurting him for no apparent reason as he was trying to get by. Danny instantly informed me of the altercation. As this wasn't the first problem we had encountered trying to get out the door, I was already at a point of frustration. I turned around, looked at Joshua, and said, "What is wrong with you?" What I meant was "what possibly could have caused you to do something like that?" He, however, answered the specific question I did ask. "I have NLD," he said, seemingly thinking I had forgotten. I have to admit his response did make me look at the situation differently, which is what we hope this book accomplishes for parents and professionals who deal with children with neurological differences.

The most frustrating aspect of having a child with neurological differences, suprisingly, has nothing to do with the child. It is trying to convince others to believe the enormity of the deficit areas faced by these children. People are more willing to believe when they can see the problem. When the problem is obvious and believable, the willingness to help is there. With these children, many of the problems are not so obvious and therefore not so believable. The presence of intelligence, talents, and other areas of strength further compound this disbelief. The most important first step you can take in improving the life of these children is believing. With believing comes a willingness to think about the world through their eyes. Along the way, you encounter people whose readiness to believe spans a continuum. Each year prior to the beginning of school, I have presented the same information to a group of teachers, and every year the results are the same. There are those who believe and work to make Joshua's life better; there are those who may or may not believe, but do no harm; and there are those who don't believe and make his life worse. I'm not sure what makes one group believe and one not. I wish there were a formula for getting everyone to believe. Unfortunately, I don't have that formula, but I am certain you can't open the door to better their life unless you believe.

As with all children, parents know their child best. I can guarantee that parents of children with neurological differences spend enormous amounts of time and energy thinking about their child and their needs. They know what works for their child and what doesn't. Most parents are more than willing to share this information with educators, professionals, coaches, group leaders, or others in any environment in which your child may find himself. More often than not, you're met with resistance from people who think they know better. They don't believe, and often choose to blatantly disregard information that has already proven to be helpful for your child. In their often well-meaning attempt to make the child independent, they insist on using techniques thought to be successful for neurotypical children. Sometimes it gets to be a struggle and confrontational because they won't believe. This results in unnecessary upset for everybody involved, including them, the family, and, most important, the child. It's exhausting and frustrating having to deal with the fallout, knowing it could all have been avoided with a little belief in the beginning. Our message here is simply, believe the parents.

Belief is the building block; the basis for all good that comes to these children. Once you believe, you can begin to work towards making their life better. Our hope is that having a system will make it easier to figure out, and inspire a desire to do so. The purpose of the STAT is to help you do just that. It's simply a tool to help you analyze their thinking and behavior, as we believe all behavior is purposeful and communicative. All behavior is meaningful. By having a system in place, you are better able to systematically think through what your child is doing, why they might be doing it, and what needs to be done.

Once you begin to ask "Why?", things get better for everyone because you are not just reacting to a behavior. Have you ever thought of a toilet as an educational opportunity? Well, Joshua did, but we didn't. At the age of three, Joshua seemed to become fascinated with flushing various items down the toilet, resulting in a back-up. This was not a one-time event. Each time this occurred Joshua's dad had to remove the entire toilet and fish out the item of the day. With each toy car, action figure, T-shirt, wash cloth, or hand towel he retrieved, the increase in his anger was obvious, but not to Joshua. We tried every explanation and punishment we knew of, certain that each one would have the desired effect of stopping that behavior. Short of flushing him, we were out of options. However, much to our astonishment, we were met with the same situation the next day. No matter what the punishment was or how often it was given, it didn't work. We never once stopped to think what was causing Joshua's behavior, we just wanted it to stop. Eventually the behavior stopped, although it was not the result of the punishment. Looking back, I believe he was trying to figure out which items would flush—a three-year-old's science experiment. Therefore, if I would have given him what he needed, which was offering an explanation about the characteristics necessary to achieve a successful flush, all the associated upset could have been avoided. It's important to remember you have a better chance of achieving your desired goal by asking why and getting to the root of the problem, as opposed to punishing the result of their behavior.

Figuring out the why of a behavior is not always easy. It takes a lot of effort and energy, often requiring continuous rethinking. The STAT organizes your thinking and presents you with the most probable areas of concern specific to children with these types of neurological differences. Step 2 of the STAT provides an overview of the most typically impacted areas, making it easier to pinpoint the cause of the problem. It's like going to the grocery store. You're much more efficient with a list than without. After developing the STAT, life got so much easier because I didn't have to rethink the potential problem areas each time an issue arose. It was a relief simply to look at the laundry list of possibilities and take an educated guess. Once you have an idea about the why, you can develop a hypothesis about their thinking or behavior and then develop a plan of action. As you use the STAT consistently, you can internalize the thinking process, allowing you to problem-solve some situations more quickly by eliminating or including possibilities.

After repeated use, you will find you are very in tune with your child's thinking, and that in and of itself can be helpful. Joshua for years has had trouble falling asleep. I assumed it was from anxiety so I dove headfirst into relaxation techniques. Thinking I had done everything I could to make it better, life continued on. Until one evening when my husband was out of town and the three boys and I decided to have a campout in my bedroom. After turning out the lights, I fell asleep and assumed everyone else had followed suit. About an hour later, I woke up and turned over to see Joshua, eyes wide open, staring at the ceiling. It looked odd; so, I continued to think about why he was laying there with his eyes wide open when he was trying to go to sleep. Following the STAT process in an attempt to gather more information, I asked him what was the first thing he did when he lay down to go to sleep. He proudly launched into what seemed like a programmed response. "I take deep breaths. Then, I relax every part of my body." Then, I replied, "Do you know that the first thing most people do is close their eyes when they try to go to sleep?" He innocently looked at me and said, "Really? Why?" I was shocked at his response, but I was happy to have found this out because the problem of falling asleep is now solved. This story illustrates two important points. First, this served as a great reminder that I do need to explain everything and not to assume he already knows. Who would think to tell someone to close his eyes in order to go to sleep? Second, I considered myself lucky to have internalized the process of the STAT. I now have a tool that makes it possible to see the world as he views it, enabling me to enhance the quality of his life.

At the end of the book you will find a STAT that can be used for quick reference. The STAT can also be used as a training device to help you teach others, such as school personnel and extended family, about your child's thinking. For instance, now when a teacher contacts me with a concern, I am able more quickly to explain Joshua's thinking and determine a possible resolution. If it is not readily apparent, I often find myself saying, "I know there's a reason, I'm just not sure what it is right now." By exposing others to this way of thinking, it's possible to transfer the skill. I was so excited one day, realizing that the ultimate goal of having other family members employ the process of the STAT had been reached. Joshua's grandpa, Gary, had strategically placed himself to be Joshua's bus driver when he was in sixth grade, making it possible for him to share many stories with me. One morning, Joshua was running late for the bus. As he saw the bus approaching, all he could think about was getting on the bus. He made it to the bus, running to the front of the line with no thought to the other children already waiting. As he positioned himself at the front, the girl behind him rolled her eyes in disgust. Joshua didn't see it, but Grandpa did. That afternoon, Grandpa seized his opportunity to repair the damage. It just so happened that Joshua and that girl were the first two on the bus. While they were waiting for the others to get on, Grandpa said to Joshua "Were you worried about missing the bus?" To which he responded, "Yeah, I was running as fast as I could." The girl chimed in, "Yeah, and you cut right in front of me." Grandpa then tried to repair the social damage by saying, "Josh, you might want to apologize because it looks like she might be mad about that." Joshua then apologized, helping to repair a potentially doomed relationship. With this knowledge, I was then able to discuss with Joshua what he could do differently next time. The countless hours my parents spent listening to me talk about the STAT process have paid off for Joshua and me, because they are now better able to see the world through his eyes.

While we've talked about the characteristics and the areas specific to children with neurological differences, it really all comes down to just a few simple guidelines:

- believe the parent
- reduce anxiety
- be kind
- check often for deep understanding
- explain everything—including things you are sure "anyone" would understand
- don't automatically assume that a negative behavior is intentional; try to determine the cause
- tell them what to do instead
- don't engage them in a power struggle
- try to see the world through their eyes
- enjoy them and laugh with them
- love them for who they are.

There are many books available that discuss specific intervention techniques to use with children with neurological differences. Our book has not been about intervention techniques. We leave that up to you to determine. Our book is a tool to determine the "why," so you can figure out what to do to meet the unique needs of your child. We have intentionally not offered specifics about what to do, because once you are able to decode the "why," the interventions will become more obvious. We hope that the information presented provides a new way for you to approach your thinking in order to help improve the life of you and your child. Ultimately, though, we want everyone who comes in contact with children with neurological differences to know how special and endearing they really are, by understanding better the way they view the world around them. To begin to achieve that goal, we must start with changing the world one person at a time.

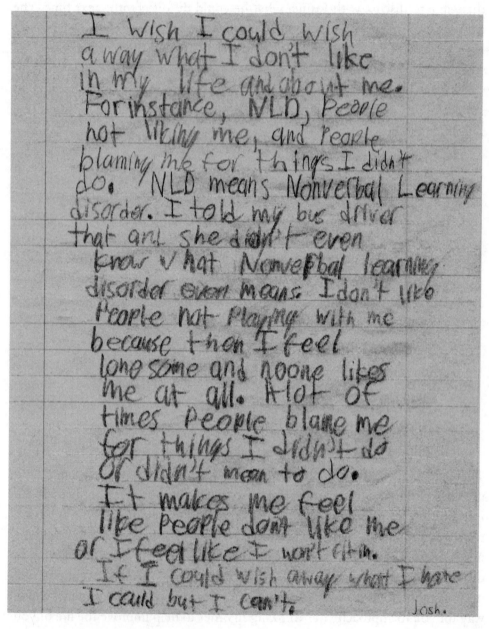

Joshua's reflections at age 10

Summary of the Systematic Tool to Analyze Thinking (STAT)

Step 1: Assess the situation

Describe the situation you want to analyze.

Step 2: Develop a hypothesis

Why? Why did they react the way they did? What could they be thinking? Select one or more of the elements below.

• Abstract language	• Motor	• Sensory	• Spatial orientation
• Control/ consistency	• Thinking about others thinking	• Social communication	• Emotions
• Mental flexibility	• Impulsive	• Executive function	• Anxiety

Hypothesis about their thinking (take a guess)—What could they be thinking to themselves? What would they be saying?

Step 3 (optional): Ask questions to obtain a step-by-step account

Types of questions

- Ask literal questions to try to prove your hypothesis.
- Ask questions that have a black and white answer.
- Ask questions that require a one or two word response.
- Provide answer choices to make it more concrete.
- Ask questions that address social cues such as body language (i.e. What did the person do that made you think that? What was she doing with her hands? etc.).

 Revise hypothesis. Go back to Step 2

Step 4: Actions to consider

Take action

Take no action

Explain

Explain and take action

Seek additional sources of help

- family members
- physician (change medication)
- neuropsychologist (further assessment)
- educators (teachers, aides, counselors, principal)
- support professionals
- parents of other children
- friends
- community resources (social groups)

Note the course of action you propose to take.

Appendix II

The Systematic Tool
to Analyze Thinking (STAT): full version

Step 1: Assess the situation

- **Describe the situation you want to analyze**
- **Determine what you know**
    - Who was there?
    - What was said?
    - What actions were taken?
    - Where did it happen?
    - When did it happen?
    - The physical and emotional state of the person—tired, emotionally vulnerable, etc.?
- **Ask questions of your child or others if more information is needed.**
    - Why did you do that?
    - Tell me exactly what happened?
    - What happened first, next, then?

Step 2: Develop a hypothesis

Why? Why did they react the way they did? What could they be thinking? Select one or more of the elements below.

Abstract language
- Literal thinking
- Figurative language/jokes, humor
- Implied/inferential
- Rhetorical questions/sarcasm
- Idioms/compound words
- Multiple meaning words
- Vocabulary
- Character development words (respect, honesty, responsibility)
- Directions/assignments

Control/consistency
- Difficulty transitioning and adapting to change
- Need to control situation so will know what will happen
- Need to rely on rules and routines
- Need schedule for predictability and to feel safe
- Often have area of special interest
- Appear rigid, directive, bossy

Mental flexibility
- Abstract vs concrete concepts
- Big picture vs focus on detail
- Focus on unimportant vs significant
- Ability to generalize or transfer skill
- Main ideas and summaries
- Cause and effect
- Understanding consequences of actions
- Prioritizing
- Editing/redoing
- Are inflexible/one right way
- Seem rude/correcting others
- Appear perfectionistic/bossy
- Thinking logical/fact oriented
- Learn by explanation and doing

Motor
- Handwriting
- Dressing (zipping, buttoning, tying shoes)
- Art (coloring, cutting)
- Eating (cutting, spilling)
- Walking, running, skipping
- Catching, throwing
- Riding a bike
- Balance/safety issues (curbs, uneven surfaces, playing equip)

Thinking about others thinking
- Theory of mind
- Perspective taking
- Empathy
- Encourage
- Consoling
- Apologizing
- Complimenting
- Compromising/negotiating
- Sharing
- Offering or asking for help
- Persuading
- Imagining or pretending
- Detecting deception (gullible)
- Understanding motive or intent
- Manners
- Explaining
- Using mental state verbs (think, know, believe)
- Understanding author's purpose/point of view
- Mood/theme
- Audience and purpose
- Forming friendships/relationships
- Working as part of group
- Are mindblind
- Are not embarrassed
- Don't lie or steal
- Don't deceive
- Are brutally honest (tell fat, bald)

Impulsivity
- Blurting out/act before think
- Consequences of actions
- Rushing through
- Waiting
- Deeper thinking
- Anticipation
- Stopping
- Excessive, exaggerated reactions

Sensory
- Sounds/tastes and textures/smells
- Touch (slapping, hugging)
- Pressure (slamming, squeezing)
- Pain tolerance/sensitivity (hypo/hyper)
- Hygiene/clothing
- Staring/eye contact
- Busy, noisy environments
- Overload

Social communication
- What to say/who to say it to
- Where, when, how to say it
- Initiate, maintain, end conversation
- Monitor understanding, repair and adjust
- Limited conversational turns/monologue
- Reading or using social cues
- Facial expressions, body language, tone
- Explain/small talk
- Speaks same way to adults as peers
- Questions (too many, too few, personal)
- Echolalia
- Friendship/dating/relationships

Executive functions
- Identify a problem
- Problem solve
- Plan
- Sequence
- Organize
- Prioritize
- Complex tasks
- Multi-step directions
- Projects
- No sense of time

Spatial orientation
- Body in space (bump into people and things, trip)
- Finding locations (lost, disoriented, late)
- Navigating environments
- Manipulating objects (pouring, placement)
- Uncoordinated/clumsy
- Maps and graphs
- Lining up numbers
- Staying in the margins
- Visually busy worksheets
- Copying from board, paper

Emotions
- Identify feelings of self or others
- Expressing own feelings
- Emotional reciprocity
- Over/understated emotional reaction
- Gradients of emotions (agitated to furious)
- Emotional intelligence
- Understanding one person can have many feelings, same event
- Understanding two people can have different emotions, same event
- Friendships/relationships
- Mood in text/inferential emotions in text
- Often look happy but not

Anxiety
- Suicide/depression
- Meltdowns/shut down
- Exhaustion/stress/fear/target for bullies
- Need for downtime/solitary time
- Need breaks
- Need reassurance, use check phrases (I'm okay?)
- Need social circles of acceptance
- Need safe interactions
- Anxiety indicators (vomiting, self-talk, twirling)

Hypothesis about their thinking (take a guess)—What could they be thinking to themselves? What would they be saying?

Step 3 (optional): Ask questions to obtain a step-by-step account

Types of questions

Ask literal questions to try to prove your hypothesis.

Ask questions that have a black-and-white answer.

Ask questions that require a one- or two-word response.

Provide answer choices to make it more concrete.

Ask questions that address social cues such as body language (i.e. What did the person do that made you think that? What was she doing with her hands? etc.).

 Revise hypothesis. Go back to Step 2

Step 4: Actions to consider

Take action

Take no action

Explain

Explain and take action

Seek additional sources of help

- family members
- physician (change medication)
- neuropsychologist (further assessment)

- educators (teachers, aides, counselors, principal)
- support professionals
- parents of other children
- friends
- community resources (social groups)

Note the course of action you propose to take.

Story Locator

Introduction

Chapter 1: The Systematic Tool to Analyze Thinking (STAT)

Chapter 2: Abstract Language

Chapter 6: Control/Consistency

Chapter 7: Thinking about Others Thinking (Theory of Mind)

Chapter 8: Social Communication

Chapter 9: Emotions

Chapter 10: Mental Flexibility

Chapter 11: Impulsivity

Chapter 12: Executive Functions

Chapter 13: Anxiety

Chapter 14: Believe

Index

abstract language
asking questions 35,
39–41
commands 31–3, 136
as a deficit area 24, 29–30
figurative language 18, 33
rhetorical questions 30–31
STAT examples 37–41
strategies 36
see also literal thinking;
misinterpretation;
vocabulary
abstract thinking 134
academic performance
and emotional
understanding 123
and impulsivity 141, 142
and mental flexibility 132
and theory of mind 91–2
see also assignments
actions to consider (STAT step
4) 26–8
"aha" moment 13, 14, 39
anxiety
about physical exercise 45
about school 161–4
control issues 74, 82–4
as a deficit area 24,
159–60
effects 165
and impulsivity 142, 144
indicators 160–61
and mental flexibility 168
and multiple deficits 165
need for breaks 163–4
and new school year 150
and social skills 163

STAT example 166–8
strategies 162–3, 166
apologizing 95, 140, 173
asking questions
precision in 35, 39–41
see also check phrases
asking questions (STAT step
3) 25–6
Asperger's see neurological
difference
assessing the situation (STAT
step 1) 21–2
assignments 32–3, 152–3
autism see neurological
difference

behavior
interpretation see systematic
tool to analyze
thinking
misunderstanding 22
behavior modification, and
inflexible thinking
134–5
belief
failure of 170
in neurological differences
14–15, 169–71
big picture, missing 132–3,
136
body language 25, 26
body in space 49, 50, 67
breaks see recess; solitary times
bullying 109–10, 161

cause and effect thinking 134,
146–7

see also consequences
change, control issues 78–9
changing register 107–8
check phrases 162
Christmas 23, 142–3, 144–6
classrooms
impulsivity problems
139–41
spatial orientation issues
66–7, 69, 70–71
clothing, sensory issues 52
clumsiness see motor control
color-coding, for school
materials 151
commands, dealing with
31–3, 136
communication skills 106–8,
114–17, 133–4
see also abstract language;
conversational skills;
echolalia; social
communication; truth
and lies
complex tasks, in assignments
153
compromise 89
computers, and social
communication 112
consequences
thinking about 143–4
see also cause and effect
thinking
consistency see control issues;
routines; rules
control issues
and anxiety 74–5, 82–4
and change 78–9